BLACK SITE

ALSO BY PHILIP MUDD

*The Head Game: High Efficiency Analytic Decision-Making
and the Art of Solving Complex Problems Quickly*

BLACK SITE

The CIA in the Post-9/11 World

PHILIP MUDD

LIVERIGHT PUBLISHING CORPORATION

A DIVISION OF W. W. NORTON & COMPANY

INDEPENDENT PUBLISHERS SINCE 1923

NEW YORK ■ LONDON

For information about permission to reproduce selections from this book,
write to Permissions, Liveright Publishing Corporation, a division of
W. W. Norton & Company, Inc., 500 Fifth Avenue, New York, NY 10110

For information about special discounts for bulk purchases, please contact
W. W. Norton Special Sales at specialsales@wwnorton.com or 800-233-4830

Manufacturing by Sheridan
Production manager: Anna Oler

Library of Congress Cataloging-in-Publication Data

Names: Mudd, Philip, author.
Title: Black site : the CIA in the post-9/11 world / Philip Mudd.
Description: First edition. | New York : Liveright Publishing Corporation, 2019.
Identifiers: LCCN 2019004545 | ISBN 9781631491979 (hardcover)
Subjects: LCSH: United States. Central Intelligence Agency—History—21st century.
| Terrorism—Prevention—Government policy—United States. |
Detention of persons—Government policy—United States. | Extraordinary
rendition—United States. | September 11 Terrorist Attacks, 2001—Influence. |
War on Terrorism, 2001–2009. | Qaida (Organization)
Classification: LCC JK468.I6 M82 2019 | DDC 327.1273009/0511—dc23
LC record available at https://lccn.loc.gov/2019004545

Liveright Publishing Corporation, 500 Fifth Avenue, New York, N.Y. 10110
www.wwnorton.com

W. W. Norton & Company Ltd., 15 Carlisle Street, London W1D 3BS

1 2 3 4 5 6 7 8 9 0

This book is for my sisters, Laura, Ellen, and Clare. Every day, we walk different paths, in different places. But the paths never seem to matter. Every day, you offer me a light. You help me make choices, you make me laugh, you help me through tough moments. You guys never fail to pull your brother along, with kindness, patience, and humor. And always love. I can try to say it, but I just can't ever thank you enough. I love you all.

CONTENTS

AUTHOR'S NOTE

This book is based largely on interviews with dozens of former Central Intelligence Agency (CIA) officers, from former CIA directors to individuals directly involved in the management and oversight of the CIA's secret detention and interrogation of al-Qa'ida prisoners. Those interviews, supplemented by readings from the literature published about the Program during the past decade, were conducted in 2015–2016, mostly in person but also by phone and Skype. I assured those officers of anonymity; where their names appear here, it was with their approval. A handful of them declined interviews. A few important players have died.

I also had personal experience in the Program, reading the intelligence derived from detainee debriefings and then, as the Counterterrorism Center's deputy director from 2003 to 2005, participating in decisions about the interrogations. The book is a third-person narrative, though. I only witnessed bits and pieces of the events described here, and shuffling in the text between my experiences and those of dozens of other officers would confuse the narrative. For the sake of maintaining a consistent third-person voice, I have avoided mixing in first-person references in the broader narrative.

This is not a history. It is a snapshot of events based on the memories and thoughts of those who were there.

PREFACE

One summer morning, as a routine repair was taking place, sparks drifted down an elevator shaft at CIA headquarters in Langley, Virginia. It wasn't long before some oily rags in the basement ignited, sending smoke back up the shaft and into the hallways and resulting in an evacuation of the buildings. This wasn't a false alarm but instead the real thing, a near-miss that would be a chance for Agency executives to study how the CIA's regularly scheduled emergency evacuation practices on the leafy northern Virginia compound would work out in a live scenario. The small fire that ensued wasn't disastrous or life-threatening, and the evacuation that followed was the type of event that might otherwise be forgotten. If not, that is, for the timing.

The Agency's response wasn't stellar. The thousands of Agency employees at the CIA's expansive Langley compound occasionally went through the motions of practice fire drills, streaming down stairwells onto sidewalks and parking lots, but those were orchestrated, and not particularly energetic. Confusion surrounded this modestly serious event, which irked the

CIA's executive director. A. B. Krongard, known universally inside and outside the Agency as "Buzzy," the senior official responsible for management at the Langley complex of buildings that make up the CIA's Headquarters compound, was in his element that day. A crusty former Marine, he liked to jokingly impress other officers with his physical fitness. But as he had helped clear the halls that day, he was underwhelmed by what he saw.

The agency quickly spearheaded an after-action study, the sort of rearview-mirror look at an event that any bureaucracy might undertake to determine how to improve policies and procedures. Krongard led the review. A veteran of the investment world and the CIA's third-ranking official, Krongard had taken a hiatus from banking to help his friend, CIA director George Tenet, rebuild a CIA that had been downsized during the post–Soviet Union budget cuts of the 1990s. Known in the Agency as the "ExDir," a shortened version of his formal title, he was the senior-most official on the business side of the Agency, responsible for everything from human resources and budgeting to emergency response.

Krongard drove the review, surely with the same relentless, no-nonsense style that characterized his blunt handling of every problem that ended up on his desk. He had a reputation as a quick decision-maker; as he later said, "I've been criticized by some who say I never met a decision I didn't like. Well, they're right."

Motivating any senior executive to focus on emergency response in peacetime isn't easy; the senior Agency officials participating in that after-action planning might have imagined that they were putting in place procedures for another fire or the snow emergencies that periodically shut down the federal government and snarled traffic around the CIA's large suburban parking lots. Those sparks spiraling down the elevator shaft, the dirty rags, the smoke, the recognition that the evacuation plan for the buildings that comprise the Agency's headquarters campus wasn't as good as it should have been—all these events happened during the late summer of 2001.

The review wasn't particularly memorable, one of a hundred priorities consuming CIA executives that summer. But, in retrospect, it was one of the inflection points that helped an Agency move from its back foot to a war footing relatively quickly. Not much prepared the CIA for the roles and responsibilities its officers assumed after the attacks. In the fall of 2001, everybody in America assumed there would be more catastrophic tragedies. It didn't seem as though anything could stop the shadowy al-Qa'ida adversary that Americans came to know overnight. Immediately afterward, the anthrax attacks hit America. Official Washington inevitably drew the conclusion that this was another al-Qa'ida attack, this time with a weapon of mass destruction, a WMD agent. Al-Qa'ida had been researching the bacteria, and the logic that they might attempt to rock the United States with an anthrax campaign immediately on the heels of 9/11 made sense. Washington was on its toes, and no one then would have guessed that the attacks were in fact tied to a disaffected American scientist. Simply put, America and the CIA were caught off-guard. Back then, everyone thought al-Qa'ida had infiltrated more terrorists in America, and that the next catastrophic attack was possible any day.

The hardest part of piecing together the memories of that period—what the Agency did, and why—centers on the insoluble problem of helping later generations understand the fears, the urgency of the moment, and the overwhelming tension surrounding the one core question: Can we move quickly enough to stop the next one? And if we don't, what are the consequences? Agency officers had to adjust to a new era of the CIA, one that shifted rapidly from an intelligence organization to a war-fighting operation.

Abu Zubaydah was perhaps the biggest riddle the Agency struggled to solve during that first year. Agency operators were accustomed to dealing in tough areas—including everything from the former Soviet Union to war zones in Africa, Latin America, and Southeast Asia—but they were not accustomed to dealing with hostile detainees. They chose to take on the new challenge, running risks that they vaguely understood but could not entirely foresee.

The CIA's overall mission also shifted, beyond the confines of detainee interrogations. Traditional intelligence typically supports war fighters from the US military, supplying them with information about the adversary's capabilities and intent as well as information about weapons systems, missile programs, and diplomatic advances. In the new counterterrorism world, the Agency was often the action arm for the information its agents collected. CIA officers gathered intelligence about al-Qa'ida leaders and then turned around and passed that information on to CIA operators who hunted down those leaders in operations that spanned the globe.

As CIA officials wrestled with the realities of this new counterterrorism landscape, accompanied by huge budget increases and vastly expanded latitude for action, they also came face-to-face with another challenge. When they began capturing senior al-Qa'ida terrorists, they were not prepared to build and manage their own prison system for the new detainees. Far from it; CIA officers had never even considered detaining prisoners as an option, and the CIA as an organization had no experience or capability in managing prisons. Nor were CIA officers recruited, trained, or practiced in dealing with recalcitrant prisoners who refused to give up the secrets that might stop the next plot.

That left the Agency with a dilemma. CIA managers felt a personal and professional responsibility to stop the next wave of al-Qa'ida killings; the prisoners they later took, in the minds of the CIA executives who ran the Agency, held clues that might stop another round of tragedy. Senior officials at the CIA correctly assumed that critics would later assail them for secret prisoners and harsh interrogations. The knot they had to untangle: either conduct the interrogations and try to break the al-Qa'ida prisoners who might hold critical intelligence clues or pass off the prisoners to another US government entity that wouldn't have the same legal authorities, clandestine mission, and willing officers to perform the interrogation mission.

Life at Langley was transformed by this expansive vision of the Agency's role. CIA officers interpreted orders from the president on down as simple: do whatever it takes to ensure this doesn't happen again. Many CIA officers also saw another reality in this mission: if the next attack happens in America, they thought, it's on us. They felt they had to do whatever it took to prevent thousands more dead. Almost anything.

In the midst of this swirling mix of new resources, legal authorities, presidential mandates, public expectations, and personal responsibility, CIA officers faced another predicament when they captured their first high-profile terrorist, Abu Zubaydah: he wouldn't talk. "We [had] to change the equation," said one of the driving forces behind the CIA's interrogation program. "I don't remember an 'aha' moment," he added, "it was just an everyday frustration. The White House was asking every day about Abu Zubaydah, and we had nothing."

What happened next has become one of the most controversial covert operations in America's history, the transfer of more than a hundred al-Qa'ida prisoners to "black sites," secret CIA prisons around the world. Even more controversial, though, was the creation and implementation of a variety of interrogation methods, called Enhanced Interrogation Techniques (or EITs) by the Agency and torture by some, that were designed to compel al-Qa'ida prisoners to speak.

These prisons, and these techniques, were often referred to by CIA officers, then and today, by two words: the Program.

Academics and journalists have long reported on and opined about the effectiveness and appropriateness of the CIA's imprisonment and harsh interrogation of prisoners. The US Senate has issued multiple formal reports about the CIA's actions, typically reports that are drafted along partisan lines. The CIA itself responded to the Senate's report with a narrow rebuttal that focused on the Senate's allegations; the rebuttal is not an explanation or description of the Program as a whole. Meanwhile, various individual CIA officers have commented on or written about their roles in the Program.

No one, however, has interviewed a broad cross section of the players involved, and no narrative compiles their views of how they decided to develop the Program; what they thought about their decisions; how they implemented this detention and interrogation program when they had little or no expertise; and what they think today about the efficacy and ethics of the now-closed detention facilities.

A decade after the CIA transferred the Program's final prisoners to the Guantanamo Bay detention facility, those officers have finally spoken through this book. I interviewed several dozen over the course of more than a year, from former directors and deputy directors to those who managed the interrogation sites from headquarters, and those who interrogated prisoners at black sites.

The most difficult part of this book has been reconstructing, for future generations, future historians, and everyday readers, what the environment was like at CIA headquarters in Langley during the dark years. History has dulled the sense of immediacy, profound threat, and pervasive responsibility CIA officers felt at that time. The CIA officers speaking today, usually anonymously, believe overwhelmingly that they were in a race against time will be lost in the debates about the Program, and in the inevitable critiques leveled by future historians. This book is an attempt to re-create that tension, but no narrative will ever fully succeed. History is better with facts than feelings.

This book is not designed to change the views of those who have drawn firm conclusions about the Program. Instead, it is an attempt to allow readers to step back in time, and to experience the world as CIA officers knew it. For both sides of the interrogation debate, the goal is the same: walk away realizing that the decisions behind this program were not easy and that oversimplifying the debate into black and white obscures what was, and still is, a morally difficult problem. The decision-makers were cognizant of the minefields they were navigating. They made choices when times were different, times that are hard to imagine today. Any observer might walk away understanding that this was a hard, and thankfully closed, chapter for America, and a unique time for its secret intelligence service.

BLACK SITE

1

The Lean Years

The Soviet Union was crumbling, and then suddenly gone. The fall of the Berlin Wall was a victory for the Central Intelligence Agency and for America. It was supposed to be the beginning of the unipolar world, with the United States at the center of global power during a time of hope for the millions of Americans who had lived under the threat of a nuclear exchange with the Soviets. It was also an era of downsizing for the US government agencies and departments that had spent decades fighting the spread of Soviet-style communism.

The Cold War had defined the Agency since its inception. The CIA traced its origins back to World War II, when the Agency's predecessor, the Office of Strategic Services (OSS), conducted sabotage behind enemy lines, collected intelligence, and supported secret opposition cells. After the war, President Harry S. Truman determined that America needed a long-term, centralized organization dedicated to fusing intelligence from various sources. This centralized federal agency would stand in contrast to the more ad hoc approach before the war that left some judging that the United States missed the Pearl Harbor warning signals from Japan because no single government organization had primary responsibility for analyzing intelligence.

The National Security Act of 1947 enshrined the new CIA as the country's focal point for collecting, disseminating, and analyzing information related to events overseas. During the 1950s, the Agency's reach grew far beyond the OSS's origins, extending to support for coups in such countries as Guatemala and Iran. Those years, at the heart of the Cold War, also led the Agency to focus its resources on the one threat that consumed America: Communism, and in particular the reach and spread of the Soviet Union.

Later decades, from the 1960s through the 1970s, brought probing questions, from how the Agency's failed Bay of Pigs operation in Cuba had gone so wrong to whether the long-term effects of US-sponsored coups were counterproductive. Iran's theocratic revolution in 1979 brought to power religious clerics who saw the United States as the backbone of the repressive regime of the Shah of Iran they despised, and the shadow of American intervention in Iranian politics during the 1950s still hangs over America's tense relationship with Tehran. Congressional probes in the 1970s, particularly the Church Committee, exposed CIA operations that included sabotage and assassinations of foreign leaders.* Those hearings heralded more congres-

---

* The committee was named for Senator Frank Church. After congressional hearings that covered the FBI, the CIA, and other federal agencies' involvement in domestic spying and overseas efforts to kill foreign leaders, the committee members issued a series of reports in 1975–76 that included recommendations for reform.

sional oversight of CIA activities and resulted in an executive order, signed by Gerald Ford, prohibiting CIA involvement in assassinations.

The veil of secrecy over the Agency that had characterized its first decades, and the congressional drive to reform the CIA, started defining Washington's attitude toward intelligence as the 1970s progressed. Through the 1980s and into the 1990s the Agency again suffered through a cycle of secret support to anti-Communist regimes followed by inquiries into how far the Agency had gone in covert assistance to sometimes brutal regimes. This culminated in the explosive investigation into the Iran-Contra affair, the illegal sale of weapons to Iran and the use of the proceeds from those sales to support Contra rebels fighting Nicaragua's leftist leaders.

And then came the Soviet collapse in 1991. The justification for a sprawling intelligence apparatus in Washington almost immediately seemed outmoded, and the aftermath of the fall was difficult for the US intelligence community. Assumptions about the end of the Soviet threat were accompanied by rosy estimates about how much the United States could save by cutting the sprawling defense industry—what Dwight Eisenhower called the "military-industrial complex"—that had grown so massively during the post–World War II years of the nuclear arms race and the global effort to blunt Communism. "Dragons and snakes," says one former CIA executive, reflecting on attitudes during the years after the fall of the Soviet Union. "We killed the dragon [the Soviet Union] at the end of the Cold War. There are only snakes left."

Through the 1980s and 1990s, even before the decline of the Soviet Union, the counterterrorism business at Langley stood alone as a different type of operating environment within the Agency. The terrorist threat to the United States overseas changed dramatically during those years, which pushed Agency executives to design a new counterterrorism program.

Lebanese Hezbollah, the Shia group backed by Iran, coordinated suicide car bombings at the US Embassy in April 1983 and the Marine barracks in Lebanon in October. The barracks attack left 299 Americans and French dead; the Embassy attack resulted in 63 deaths, among them CIA personnel including one of the Agency's legendary Middle East specialists, Robert Ames.

The Embassy bombing, at that point the deadliest attack on a US mission overseas, involved a bomb-laden van detonated by a suicide strike inside the Embassy. The barracks bombing, following so soon after, led to a US pullout of troops that had been part of an international presence installed to keep the peace among fighting factions in Lebanon's civil war. The language of the time gave Americans a taste of the gap between their perception of the United States—a power that would intervene on the side of the good overseas—and local perceptions, where Washington's influence and the US Marines' presence was viewed as siding with one Lebanese faction over others in the country's fractured political scene. America was part of a "crusader presence," read one statement issued by the terrorists after the attacks.

Suicide bombings were a new phenomenon, and hostage takings soon also became prevalent in Lebanon. In March 1984, just a year after the Embassy and Marine barracks attacks, Hezbollah kidnapped William Buckley, the CIA's station chief in Lebanon, dragging him from his car at gunpoint as he left his apartment building.

Buckley's body wasn't recovered for six years after his killing, when an anonymous caller gave police directions to a body dumped near Beirut Airport. Medical and dental records provided the evidence necessary for his identification, and his body came home in a flag-draped coffin. These events hit particularly close to home at CIA headquarters.

Buckley's death became one of the foundational events that led the Agency's leaders to concentrate attention on terrorism, starting during the Reagan years. In 1986, the Agency reorganized to fight this new threat, designing a different bureaucratic structure to counter Hezbollah. The Counterterrorism (originally Counterterrorist) Center (CTC) was born, evolving over time to combat a variety of threats that later came to include not only Shia Hezbollah but also Sunni groups, particularly al-Qa'ida. The counterterrorism mission was unique back then, housed in a group at the Agency that broke down barriers. CTC analysts and field managers sat side by side, a physical partnership at Langley that was anathema in other areas. Indeed, the Agency had historically separated the two. Field operators, the men and women who recruited and ran secret agents overseas, were isolated from the analysts, the men and women who read the secret field reports, coupled them with other intelligence data such as intercepted communications and foreign media reports, and wrote intelligence articles for Washington policymakers about global events.

Although analysts and operators alike all held the same Top Secret security clearances, the highest in government, the intelligence material handled by operations specialists was deemed so sensitive—because, for example, it might identify a human source inside a foreign government—that the analysts were provided it only on a "need-to-know" basis. In the kind of arcane hierarchy that defines all bureaucracies but is understood only by those on the inside, the field operators also wielded the most firepower in the Agency.

The analysts were partners, with their own proud distinctions and history, but they couldn't match the Agency's operational wing for bureaucratic and budgetary heft. Guards sat at the Agency's elevator banks, checking codes on the badges that Agency employees were required to display above the waistline. Some elevators led to the Agency's operational divisions; others to analytic divisions. Analysts were blocked from the operational elevator banks in a byzantine, outdated organizational model that the CTC broke.

This culture of jointness was driven by one of the most powerful directors in Agency history, the legendary William J. "Bill" Casey, a New York lawyer, longtime adviser to Ronald Reagan, and one-time member of clandestine operations in World War II by the CIA's predecessor organization. His tenure included controversial operations to aid anti-Communist guerrillas, and he also became embroiled in the biggest scandal of the Reagan presidency, the Iran-Contra scandal.* His reputation stemmed partly from his unusual presence: balding with a fringe of white hair, stooped, and known for rumpled suits, he mumbled through

---

* In the mid-1980s, during the administration of President Reagan, CIA officers including Casey worked with the White House in a secret plan to sell arms to the Iranian regime and use the proceeds to fund Contra rebels in Nicaragua. At that time, after the Iranian revolution in 1979 and abduction of American hostages in Lebanon by the Iran-backed Hezbollah organization, arms sales to Iran were proscribed. Further, Congress had proscribed support for the Contras, so the White House plan, with CIA support, violated both the Iran embargo and the congressional prohibition on Contra support. Casey died in the midst of the scandal, but two CIA officers were later indicted. Reagan pardoned them and others involved in the plan.

so many meetings that his incomprehensible comments were known throughout the building as his trademark.

Casey's commitment to anti-Communist operations was as consistent as his drive to restructure counterterrorism. Many Agency managers initially resisted the changes he mandated in forcing operations staff and analysts together, but he never wavered. He wasn't a classic leader—he often left subordinates guessing about his words and his intentions—but he drove change. He used his memorably obscure speaking style and his closeness to the White House, "the Casey myth," as a key leadership advantage for an Agency that prided itself on providing intelligence and counsel to the highest levels of government. If there was somebody willing to take on challenges, including fighting a hidebound bureaucracy, it was Casey. The bureaucracy didn't make him, he made the bureaucracy. Over time, both sides of the CIA house, the operators and the analysts, buckled under Casey's pressure. All the kicking and screaming about feared security breaches disappeared, though not immediately.*

CTC maintained its unique status as a combined enterprise of analysts and operators despite dramatic changes in the terror threat overseas that started during the early 1990s. In retrospect, the attacks of that decade seem like a series of unmistakable

---

* Managers initially tried to stitch together a hybrid system, sending analysts to CTC but managing them from another analytic center in the Agency. Over time, though, that interim step gave way to a full-fledged partnership between analysts and field operators in the Center, and the partnership worked. Some analysts at other offices in Langley still focused on long-term strategic assessments. In a shift that is still evident today, though, one senior manager who witnessed those changes described the new style of counterterrorism work, particularly for analysts: "CTC needed unique, time-sensitive work. Over time, the tether of CTC analysts to a traditional office proved unworkable." The joint model in CTC endured.

wake-up calls for the new terrorism, the shift from the Iranian-sponsored Hezbollah organization that represented terrorism from the Shia branch of Islam to more amorphous, independent Sunni groups that had little or no sponsorship from any state. Starting with the 1993 attack in New York at the World Trade Center site, the decade also then witnessed 19 dead in a truck bombing at the Khobar Towers building in Saudi Arabia; followed by the downtown Oklahoma City bombings at a federal government building in 1995, when 168 people died in a massive bomb blast. Whether it was al-Qa'ida in New York and Africa; Iran in Saudi Arabia; or antigovernment extremists in Oklahoma, no national security official could ignore the insistent drumbeat of terrorism.

The World Trade Center attack in 1993 marked a seminal moment that set the tone for CTC's growing focus on Sunni Muslim extremists, in contrast to the Shia terrorists who had killed Buckley and other Americans in Lebanon during the 1980s. The intent of the attack presaged 9/11: the plotters intended to use a huge improvised explosive device in a rented van to buckle one of the two World Trade Center towers, potentially downing the building and collapsing the neighboring structure at the same time. The truck bomb detonated and killed six but failed to result in crippling structural damage. One of the conspirators, Ramzi Yousef, was the nephew of Khalid Shaykh Mohammed, the architect of the 9/11 attacks.

Despite these turning points in the world of terrorism, the Agency didn't assign top priority to the counterterrorism mission. That changed quickly when George Tenet was appointed director of the CIA in 1997 and prioritized counterterrorism. Implementing his priorities, though, took time and effort. One senior manager who transferred to CTC's front office at the time says his experience reflected the second-tier status of counterterrorism then. People called him from all over the Agency, asking, "What are you doing? That's a dying issue."

Tenet's focus on terrorism kept the issue not only alive but prominent. He had come into the job young; born in 1951 to a working-class Greek family in Queens, he was a busboy in the family diner before receiving degrees from Georgetown University and Columbia University. In 1982 he joined the Senate as a staff member; he became a member of the Senate Select Committee on Intelligence in 1985, working under influential senators who later helped vault him into the highest echelons of American intelligence. Tenet was appointed the CIA's deputy director in 1995 and rose to become director only two years later, an almost meteoric ascent in Washington. His experience as a senior congressional staff member and his post as the National Security Council's intelligence adviser gave him contacts and insights into intelligence coming into the job. His voracious appetite for intelligence once he joined the Agency allowed him to grasp the business in depth.

Tenet's larger-than-life personality—boisterous, collegial, joking, profane, at times mercurial—contributed to his acceptance in the workforce. He would drink coffee at a table in the main cafeteria, chat with a junior officer, or play in the CIA basketball league with staff. He dove into work, machine-gunning questions at the same time that he learned the names of subordinates and their subordinates, and details about their lives and interests outside the office.

He could be up one day and down the next, critical of Agency analysts and operators but also their cheerleader, frustrated and remarkably supportive. Throughout the Agency, though, he was viewed by many, senior and junior officers alike, as a director who had a rare combination of talents: he had access to the Oval Office and presidents Bill Clinton and George W. Bush that was more frequent than most directors; he respected the workforce; and he lived and breathed intelligence. Even on summer vacations, he would mark up memos in a distinctive thick blue felt-tip marker, sending back questions and demands that sometimes led CIA officials to view his vacation queries as more demanding than his incessant in-person poking and prodding.

Tenet's drive on terrorism came as stories emerged of a shadowy extremist who was funding the growing al-Qa'ida. That hazy figure? Osama bin Ladin. The Agency had initially known of bin Ladin partly because of how he mixed in radical circles that swirled in Sudan and also because bin Ladin and his followers publicly announced their intentions toward America. Then, in 1996, the first of two bin Ladin religious documents appeared, the "Declaration of War Against the Americans Occupying the Land of the Two Holy Places," a reference to the US troops in Saudi Arabia, the home of the two holiest locations in Islam. Two years later, bin Ladin and a small group of followers calling themselves the World Islamic Front issued another religious decree, "Jihad Against Jews and Crusaders," calling on Muslims to take responsibility for attacking Americans and their allies anywhere in the world. In other words, Al-Qa'ida was openly declaring war on the West.

CTC's position in the Agency endured and grew not just because of al-Qa'ida's emergence and Tenet's drive and attention but also because the culture within the Center, and its reputation across the Agency, were maturing. In particular, leadership changes in the Center meant that its stock was rising at the Agency, especially given the support of Tenet. Spotting, assessing, developing, recruiting, and handling "assets"—a CIA term for the foreign informants on the payroll—was the bread and butter of the CIA's overseas officers.

Late in the decade, CTC brought in a Center director who was viewed, among those crucial operations officers, as a serious player. His transfer was yet another move that could have been straight from a management textbook: transfer an organizational heavyweight to a part of the organization you want to build and that heavyweight can change perceptions.

Cofer Black, the new CTC director, was determined to help the center go on the offensive in the counterterror campaign. "Taking the fight to the enemy," he called it.

Black was legendary in counterterrorism circles at the CIA for his long career in tough assignments and his personal involvement at the center of one of the most storied counterterrorism takedowns in history, the capture of Carlos the Jackal in Sudan in 1994.* Black's personality was tough, and sometimes dramatic, and his large stature matched his operational reputation. Like Tenet, he was passionately committed to the counterterrorism mission before 9/11, pressing for more action among policymakers in Washington, pushing foreign intelligence services overseas, and overshadowing his peers at the CIA's headquarters. He and Tenet were like-minded, and Tenet often bypassed bureaucracy to work with people who shared his vision and views. For some in the chain of command, it seemed like he was cutting them out, but that was Tenet's way.

Energetic in speech, unafraid of confronting colleagues, and

---

* Carlos the Jackal (Ilich Ramirez Sanchez) was convicted in France for a series of murders and terror strikes there in the 1970s. He was captured in Sudan in 1994 in a joint intelligence operation that included American intelligence assistance and then deported to France for trial. He remains imprisoned in France.

aggressive in his operational approach, Black was a tailor-made counterpart for the colorful Tenet. Black set CTC on an upward path before the attacks, with Tenet always in the background supporting the CTC director as he battled for resources and carved out a profile in White House meetings. Tenet didn't mind aggressiveness, he encouraged it. Black complied.

Setting an aggressive tone for CTC, Black used the CTC budget during the lean years of the 1990s as leverage with other, more traditional, operational components in the Agency. One of CTC's challenges had been the fact that it did not control any CIA offices overseas, so its senior managers could not offer up-and-coming operations officers management jobs overseas. Those plum assignments were controlled by the traditional divisions that had responsibility for Asia, Africa, Europe, Latin America—all the world's major geographic regions. Black changed that. He used the money CTC received to fund and help manage several international offices, an unheard-of coup for an Agency entity that had been seen as a minor-league player.

He also changed CTC's recruitment of a new generation of operations officers. In what was a CIA ritual that seemed more like a fraternity pledging experience than a bureaucratic exercise, the Agency's operations managers regularly traveled to the CIA's main training facility, a sprawling expanse of land called "the Farm," to mix with the new trainees and determine which of them to try to recruit into individual divisions. CTC didn't have a seat at this draft table for new talent. Black changed that, though, pushing to participate in the direct recruitment of the new graduates. He added relevance—"gravitas," as one officer put it—to a Center that had been an Agency stepchild since its inception in 1986. As this officer who worked for Black described it, "Cofer gave CTC an operational centering. He made it a player." He describes the shifting attitudes: "If you want a cool ops [operational] job, come to CTC."

Al-Qa'ida's relentless march matched CTC's emergence. The terror events through the late 1990s showed that bin Ladin's stewing rage, expressed in ideological statements, would not be empty words. The 1998 attacks against American embassies in Kenya and Tanzania left more than two hundred dead, by far the biggest loss of life since Hezbollah had burst on the scene. Meanwhile, an almost-forgotten event in America kept the CTC team working and solidified its status within the Agency during these years and into the new century. It was the long search for Mir Aimal Kansi, who murdered two CIA employees and wounded three others in a shooting outside a CIA entrance in January 1993. Kansi had purchased an automatic weapon and stopped his car at a stoplight directly outside CIA headquarters. Stepping outside his car, he calmly murdered two CIA staff and injured three others. Kansi fled overseas immediately after the killings, and it took local investigators days to center on him as the primary suspect. He returned home to his native Pakistan.

Quickly, Kansi became the subject of a massive manhunt that was to last four years, paralleling that 1990s' era of the early emergence of al-Qa'ida. CTC assembled a group to work with the FBI to find intelligence about Kansi's whereabouts, but the project was defined by fits and starts. False leads, operations that never bore fruit, and endless dead ends in Pakistan meant that the trail occasionally went cold, even as it proved exhaustive and extensive. Says one CTC manager who was involved in overseeing the operation, "We never stopped probing, including would-be snatch operations when we thought we had him located."

None of this panned out until 1997. "The final operation had nothing to do with anything that preceded it," the manager remembers. "The [informant] shows up in Karachi, says I can get him [Kansi]." The informant carried a photograph of Kansi, who was using an alias; the photo appeared to be a match. The combination of Kansi's murder of CIA officers and the CIA's partnership with the FBI in the hunt for him meant that he remained a top-tier priority for the Agency while he was on the run. Kansi, captured in a swiftly developing operation, soon came back to America on a US government aircraft, to be tried and then executed.

The Kansi case, beginning the same year as the fateful first attack on the World Trade Center, galvanized the Agency. Catching him was a "big deal for us," remembers a senior CTC manager. The case was a stunning operational coup.

The FBI was key to the Kansi hunt particularly because of the law-enforcement focus of US counterterrorism operations then and the interest in bringing Kansi back to a US court for trial. The CIA typically collects information for intelligence purposes, to help inform and guide US policymakers, but that information is not collected and processed in a manner that is designed for US courts. CIA intelligence is not evidence. The FBI does, however, collect evidence, ensuring that a chain of custody is defensible in court, for example, and that evidentiary standards can withstand questioning by a defense lawyer who can probe every bit of the prosecution's case in an open hearing. Further, FBI agents, in addition to their expertise in evidence collection, are far more likely to appear in court as witnesses in public trials than CIA officers. To bring Kansi to trial, and to collect the evidence needed to convict him, FBI partnership in the hunt was critical.

For years, FBI agents worked the case, both from FBI offices in Washington and also through FBI representatives who were on long-term assignments to the Counterterrorism Center at the CIA. Those agents sat in on CTC meetings to trade information and ensure that FBI agents at Bureau headquarters and field offices had a pipeline into the CIA. FBI partnership wasn't perfect, by any means, across the CIA, but the ties were strong on the Kansi case. There would be no prospect of an endgame—justice meted out in a US federal court—without FBI agents working side-by-side with the Agency, so it wasn't just a partnership built on some polite sense of goodwill, it was a link cemented by need.

After the capture, Tenet hosted a raucous event in the Agency "bubble"—the large auditorium on the CIA's campus—to commemorate and celebrate the partnership with the Bureau. It was one of the high-water marks in CIA-FBI cooperation before 9/11, with a CIA audience cheering the FBI agents who were part of the core of the Kansi takedown. The operation also bore the hallmarks of the limitations of counterterrorism operations, though. One CTC manager from that period recalls, "A military transport aircraft was in the region. They diverted it to pick up Kansi and flew to Dulles. Then they sent a multimillion dollar bill to the FBI to cover the cost."

Kansi and other operations kept the world of counterterrorism afloat, but the rest of the Agency had critical needs during the down decade of the 1990s. Training was one. At the main CIA training facility, cuts had left the program gutted, says one senior staff officer from that period. "Around 1995," he recalls, "we only sent a few dozen people [operations officers destined for overseas posts] through the Farm. It was a disaster, in terms of infrastructure, staffing, and funds. It hadn't been touched in years. Tenet put in the works an effort. We didn't have a lot of money, but the training numbers rose sharply [later in the 1990s]." In other words, the CIA budget was waning, but internally the Agency was at least focusing more attention on increasing the numbers of people dedicated to training for overseas operations.

Another initiative, funding for the Northern Alliance, the anti-Taliban force that would prove so critical after 9/11, also continued during the latter part of the 1990s, a forgotten investment from those years that paid huge dividends later. Says the same officer, "Continuing to support the Northern Alliance was absolutely key. There was controversy around that. Nobody could figure out why we did it. But it didn't cost a lot. Tenet and the guys in NE [the CIA's Near East Division, the element responsible for operations in Afghanistan] deserve a lot of credit."

2

Risk Avoidance

As the CTC developed at Langley, so too did the Agency's field operations overseas against terrorists. Like the limited expansions at CIA headquarters, though, field operations were constrained by budgetary limitations and, more significantly, the hesitation of US officials to attack al-Qa'ida head on, especially with operations that risked loss of life. The budgetary tightening resulted from another of the key global events of the 1990s: the fall of the Berlin wall remained a key driver of US intelligence policy. Through the mid-1990s, the US intelligence community was enduring the downsizing of the peace-dividend era. CTC wasn't spared budget and personnel cuts, even if the Center was better insulated than other Agency departments.

In one example of the pre-attack limitations, a senior Agency operator from the late 1990s remembers the Center spending half a year putting together the plan to acquire a transport helicopter for use among CIA-supported Afghans. Because of the lengthy

Russian intervention into Afghanistan during 1979–89, when the Russian Army invaded to back the Communist government in Kabul, foreign equipment in Afghanistan (and in the neighboring Central Asian states, formerly part of the Soviet Union) was common. Further, Americans supporting the Afghan militias wanted "plausible deniability," the ability to deny any formal US government support for the guerrillas, so use of a US military helicopter would have been unacceptable. In those days, that acquisition—especially considering the price tag—was seen as a significant success. Later, CTC's budget and acquisitions would dwarf that purchase, in money spent and speed of acquisition. One helicopter would be an afterthought.

There are now-forgotten pointers to how the boxed-in operators worked within tight constraints. Perhaps the most significant planning exercise was to take out Osama bin Ladin, orchestrated in the few years before 9/11. Bin Ladin had slowly come into focus after his early years in Sudan and his expulsion to Afghanistan in 1996, partly as a result of American pressure on the Sudanese government. Once in Afghanistan, he was an elusive target for the Agency. Soft-spoken and inspirational to his followers, he built an organization around him based partly on his devotion to his version of extreme Islam, his perceived piety and simplicity, and his commitment not only to speak of ridding Muslim lands from Western influence but also to act, most notably with the 1998 attacks.

He also built his support base with money, though how much he had was never clear. The son of an extremely wealthy businessman who had parlayed close links with the Saudi royal family into an extensive construction empire, bin Ladin inherited wealth that fueled the cash-strapped extremists with whom he circulated. Money, activism, humility—between the early 1990s and 1998 he transitioned in the eyes of the Agency from a donor to one of the world's most dangerous terrorists. Finally he was prominent enough that the FBI placed him on its Most Wanted list in 1999 (he remained on the list until his death in 2011), and the US government put a $25 million price on his head.

To get closer to bin Ladin, the Agency had cultivated a group of local Afghans to collect intelligence on him and al-Qa'ida inside Afghanistan. They helped identify bin Ladin's location with enough specificity to stage a capture and then shift bin Ladin to an airfield in southern Afghanistan for transport to US authorities.

No CIA officer thought the scheme had more than a slim prospect of success. Because the CIA wasn't authorized to design an operation with the expressed intent to kill bin Ladin, they had to come up with a scenario to use the group as a capture team, relying on the group to fight bin Ladin's guards, capture the al-Qa'ida chief, transport him to an airfield, and wait until a US team could arrive to whisk him away. In a show of just how limited their options were, though, CIA officers briefed this operation to Cabinet-level officials in Washington. Said one former senior manager, "They were a joke. It was the Barney Fife of counterterrorism. But they were one of the only things we had, other than satellites." This wasn't a universal view, but it summarizes some senior officials' perspective.

The policy boundaries that surrounded the options for taking bin Ladin down, though, were as constraining as the local group's own limitations. Al-Qa'ida's large Tarnak Farm facility in southern Afghanistan, a well-known center for the group's operations and a site bin Ladin occasionally visited, was a key focus for intelligence collection during the 1990s. The collection had a simple motive: could the CIA, and other US government intelligence agencies, locate bin Ladin with enough precision to raise the likelihood of a successful strike? And, equally important, could the Agency collect intelligence that was sufficiently precise to ensure little or no civilian loss of life?

On the surface, these questions seem simple. Within the answer, though, lies the complex world of Washington decision-making—the web of risk calculations—that post-9/11-attack CIA officers were so driven to move beyond. First, there was the question of policy documentation. Some of the original presidential guidance on terrorism dated from the Reagan presidency, and it was simply constructed. Later, senior officials from successive administrations through George H. W. Bush and Bill Clinton, including White House advisers and their CIA counterparts, added details that might have eliminated gray areas but also layered on cumbersome restrictions that virtually guaranteed there would never be a successful operation against bin Ladin before 9/11. "Rules of engagement"—that is, how US teams could engage with potential al-Qa'ida adversaries short of targeting them for killing—became tighter.

Any covert action conducted by the Agency must, by law, stem from a presidential authorization, called a finding. The president issues a formal order; the CIA then executes the order and reports formally to Congress on the covert action. Said one senior CIA official involved in reviewing the documents, "These MOUs [Memoranda of Understanding] could be twenty pages long, filled with what ifs, whereases." The threat was never immediate enough to cut the layers of bureaucratic language.

Those "what ifs" significantly added to the complexity of the rules the CIA would have to follow to execute an operation against bin Ladin. What if potential captors come under fire? What are the circumstances under which you could contemplate killing al-Qa'ida members if you tried a raid on bin Ladin? What constituted sufficient "eyes on" the target to have a level of confidence that bin Ladin was actually at the compound? Scenario after scenario, all designed to ensure that America wasn't in the assassination game, and that capture and prosecution was the priority. This mentality infused the al-Qa'ida targeting process before the 9/11 attacks—the constant effort to limit risk. "It was ridiculous," remembers one former senior CIA manager. Others are less harsh, but they all characterize the pre-9/11 conditions for engaging al-Qa'ida as light-years different than what followed.

In the end, the boundaries on how the CIA could consider a raid against bin Ladin and al-Qa'ida at Tarnak Farms ensured that there wouldn't be an operation. The local group couldn't come up with precise intelligence or design an operation that would be clean enough to promise a decent probability of a capture operation rather than a kill operation. Further, the escalating Washington discussions about what would constitute "eyes on" target—in other words, what Washington would accept as confirmation that bin Ladin was where the Agency thought he was—set a bar for confirmation that the Agency couldn't meet. It wasn't that they never had information on bin Ladin's location, including spotting him with an unarmed drone. It was that reaching a level of certitude about where he would be tomorrow was simply a bridge too far.

Similar to the snatch conversations, discussions about using long-range missiles—Tomahawk Land Attack Missiles, long-range cruise missiles better known by the acronym TLAMs—were bounded by understandable, but onerous, constraints. To argue for direct action against bin Ladin, an operation the White House would have to authorize, the CIA needed to provide assurances on a combination of questions that minimized risk to a level that almost guaranteed no missile would ever be launched. They needed precision on bin Ladin's location, with enough advance notice that the missiles could launch and hit the target. And, of course, they'd need some assurance that bin Ladin would still be there. Lastly, they needed him to be in a location that eliminated the prospect of loss of life among innocent civilians. There was also a thorny diplomatic question: What, if anything, do you tell any country if a TLAM is going to overfly their airspace? Should the United States provide warning even if its diplomats didn't request approval?

The TLAM timelines were too long. An operator planning a missile strike would have to start by assuming a few hours to transmit the order to a submarine in the Indian Ocean. Add another few hours for missiles loaded and fired from that submarine to hit a distant target. Already, the likelihood that perishable intelligence about the location of al-Qa'ida's skittish and security-conscious leader would allow a four-hour lead time, or more, seemed remote. That timeline would come only after senior officials would review the intelligence for approval. There is a term of art in the intelligence business: "actionable," meaning intelligence that allows a policymaker to make an informed decision. With these rules, the likelihood that the CIA could develop intelligence to provide advance warning of bin Ladin's whereabouts with enough time and certainty to meet policymakers' "actionable" requirements—to give them such a long lead-time to make a decision—was low.

Some in the Agency still didn't see this unlikely pre-9/11 authorization scenario as a hopeless exercise, though. They persisted. Agency officials had an idea of which locations in Afghanistan might be on bin Ladin's travel circuit, so they pieced together target packages, on each of a handful of locations, and passed them out to the senior officials who would be involved in the strike authorization. Instead of wasting time briefing a group of officials on a strike site, they could just say, "He's at Site One."

It stretches credulity today to imagine that this byzantine

approval process would ever come into play, given the lead times required for a strike. But one former senior officer says it did, as bin Ladin began capturing the attention of US policymakers before 9/11. In one example, in the late 1990s, intelligence from the CIA's network of Afghans indicated that bin Ladin might be at a compound in southern Afghanistan for an overnight stay, and perhaps through the following morning's prayers. The targeting process started, but quickly the policy straitjacket of eliminating risk drove the process. First, American intelligence could never get eyes on target, particularly Americans on the ground confirming that bin Ladin was there when the Afghan informant network said he would be there. And second, satellite imagery identified a mosque nearby. The cruise missiles aimed at the site would have reduced the buildings to dust; they might also have sparked an international outcry if the strikes damaged the mosque. The operation never happened.

The policy focus on weighing different options to strike al-Qa'ida or snatch bin Ladin extended to some of the most senior levels in Washington's national security apparatus, but the attention to the terror problem didn't resolve the key question of whether Washington was doing enough to get in front of a new brand of global terror. Tenet raised plans created by CTC's bin Ladin unit, but there was "an endless series of questions" from policy advisers, says the Tenet adviser. "The politics of the situation and the natural hesitancy means that it [the CIA operational proposals] was never good enough." For their part, the CIA's access also wasn't good enough to come up with actionable options. One of the senior operators from that era captures the environment: "We [the US government] were risk averse."

It wasn't as if they didn't discuss risk often with the White House. Tenet's regular sessions included Sandy Berger, who was critical in Tenet's engagement with the White House. A longtime Clinton aide, he served as National Security Adviser from 1997 through the end of the Clinton presidency, and he played key roles in the many national security turning points of the decade, from negotiating peace between factions in Northern Ireland to working on the Dayton Accords to ending fighting in Bosnia and pressing for White House engagement to prevent an escalation of tensions between India and Pakistan. Meanwhile, he was Tenet's go-to person in the White House for al-Qa'ida conversations leading up to the Bush transition in January 2001.

Underneath Berger was the longtime White House counterterrorism czar Richard Clarke. An often infuriating presence prodding various Washington agencies, including the CIA, Clarke was demanding and abrasive, with an over-the-top personality. Regardless of his well-known flaws, though, many intelligence officers reflecting back decades after their engagement with Clarke now see his preparations leading into the new century as positive. Even as they acknowledge that Clarke's insistent direction was often rough—Clarke was known for sharp elbows and blunt language—the White House relationship with the Agency was close, even symbiotic. Clarke needed somebody to take his aggressiveness and try to operationalize it. The CIA's Counterterrorism Center was the government entity to which he often turned.

These White House officials talked with CIA officers about what might happen if things changed dramatically. They stepped through what they called "blue-sky" planning with the White House to prepare for a day when they might receive more aggressive, expansive counterterrorism authorities. CIA officers then didn't expect that even a notional mandate would leave the Agency holding prisoners. Instead, they judged that in the event the US government captured and held prisoners, the US military would be the right agency to hold them. The military had detention experience, resources, and expertise in interrogations and interrogation training. The Agency didn't, and the problems posed by some expanded detainee program seemed bigger than the Agency, which is dwarfed by the US military. As one officer said of attitudes across government in the 1990s, "People thought, 'We don't need the Agency. We need the Peace Corps.'" Another pointed out the contrast between the go-go atmosphere of post-9/11 Langley and the criticisms that the Agency hadn't done enough before the attacks. "After 9/11, the attitude was, 'put their heads on stakes,' and people forgot how conservative the environment was before the attacks." One senior CTC manager who participated in this blue-sky thinking remembers his clear thoughts on some of the ideas that would later become commonplace at the CIA: "Before 9/11, this was all just larger than us."

The ripple effect of historical events from the 1990s helps explain some of this policy reticence in the years preceding the attacks. A senior CIA officer reflecting on that period sees the Washington caution through the lens of the humanitarian operation in Somalia that had gone so wrong during the Clinton presidency. A US government effort to provide aid to Somalia, riven by a civil war among tribal factions, resulted in the deployment of US forces. In October 1993, in the midst of that humanitarian effort, Somali militants downed two helicopters in attacks that left eighteen servicemen dead. Horrific scenes of the attackers dragging several dead Americans through the streets of the Somali capital, Mogadishu, appeared in American media. One CIA officer involved in counterterrorism operations after 9/11 says American decision- makers recoiled from a potential replay of the Black Hawk episode; no president would want two such catastrophes on his resume. Another CTC executive from that time referred to a second military episode to explain American policy reticence. "There was a low tolerance for missions that would be seen like the Desert One failure," he says, referring to the ill-fated military operation to rescue American hostages in Iran in April 1980 that resulted in an embarrassing operational disaster.*

Drones were among those areas where policy reticence proved decisive. Before 9/11, US government officials foot-dragged on the controversial policy decision to arm Predator drones. Instead, the unmanned aircraft served only as collection systems, pilotless cameras in the sky unique in their ability to dwell over locations for extended periods. An unarmed Predator had taken footage of "the tall guy," recalls one senior CTC manager referencing video of a figure many thought was bin Ladin, but there was no agreement that using an armed drone against him was acceptable, or even who would manage such a mission in the US government. Even now, senior officers bristle at the suggestion that intelligence collection against al-Qa'ida was weak. They often point instead to missed opportunities, and to the limitations within which they worked. When bin Ladin appeared on Predator drone footage, for example, officers now lament that the Agency, and the US government generally, had few options and little will to respond quickly to that fleeting intelligence picture. This incident highlights their view that intelligence collection was good enough to identify the adversary: an armed drone then, they say, would have eliminated bin Ladin.

Meanwhile, bin Ladin was homing in on America. As if to

---

* President Jimmy Carter ordered a US military operation in 1980 to rescue fifty-two embassy personnel who had been taken hostage by Iran and held in Tehran after the Iranian revolution in 1979. The operation, including eight helicopters, was aborted after several helicopters failed. One helicopter hit a transport aircraft, leaving eight servicemen dead.

remind CTC officers of al-Qa'ida's persistence, and the reality
the millennium threat, an al-Qa'ida plotter was arrested imm
diately before the New Year's celebrations. Ahmed Ressam,
thirty-four-year-old Algerian, attempted to enter Washingto
State from Canada. His background was textbook al-Qa'ida: h
eventually found his way to Canada, where he met an al-Qa'ida
recruit who had trained in Afghanistan and persuaded Ressam
to follow the same path. Ressam did, and he returned to Canada
with an explosives background and instructions. He assembled
timing devices and mixed explosives, aiming to head across the
border into Washington State and then down to Los Angeles.

Ressam nearly succeeded. In a remarkable twist of fate, an
alert US official at the border decided on a secondary inspection
of Ressam's rental vehicle, based not on intelligence but on an
experienced hunch. That hunch turned out to be correct. Hid-
den in the trunk of the vehicle were the materials he would need
to build an improvised explosive device. Later, he admitted that
his target was Los Angeles International Airport, a prominent
economic target, in the midst of America's celebrations, which
he planned to bomb on New Year's Eve, 1999.

Ressam himself, in testimony, reinforced CTC officers'
views, and those of a deeply disturbed CIA director, that the
Millennium plot was real.

Q. Did you discuss the type of target you would pick in the
   United States?
A. [Ressam]. Yes.
Q. What was that discussion?
A. The discussion was about an airport, an airport, a con-
   sulate, that's what I remember.
Q. Were you aware of plans being made by other groups in
   the camp as well?

A. Yes, there were others who were planning other than us.

Q. Generally, what did you know about what the other groups were doing?

A. To carry out operations in Europe, in the Gulf, against US and Israel.

Q. What was the timing of those operations?

A. Before the year 2000.

Time ran out for the Clinton team to address al-Qa'ida and the potential for future Ressam-like threats, though it's hard to imagine any approach would have been aggressive enough to counter al-Qa'ida in its remote safe haven in Afghanistan. The White House, under National Security Adviser Berger, had ordered up the blue-sky memos in the waning period of the Clinton presidency. Berger was focused on the al-Qa'ida threat; a presidency that had hoped to reap the benefits of the post-Soviet peace dividend also had faced the new reality of so many terror attacks during the 1990s. But presidencies don't turn on dimes in their waning months. To put in place a major sea change in the hunt for al-Qa'ida would have taken political capital. And time. The blue-sky thinking lacked both.

During the first months of the Bush presidency, the White House and other officials in the national security world were focused on one priority: missile defense against emerging adversaries such as Iran and North Korea. From the White House to Secretary Rumsfeld at the Department of Defense, the specter of foreign foes acquiring missiles that could strike America was sparking a national debate about how to build American missile defenses. CIA officials knew they were sometimes seen as pounding the table on their own hobbyhorse: terrorism. Further, they thought other agencies in the defense world viewed their

rumblings about hazy terror plots as money-grab attempts after an era of cuts in national security programs.

The Agency officers also believed they were viewed as doomsayers who were "covering their asses," as some said, by talking about plots that never happened. In early August the CIA published an item in the President's Daily Brief, the flagship CIA publication that offered intelligence updates to the president and his top advisers. That article talked of plots against America. The reaction of the president seemed clear; the message back to the CIA was that Agency officers were providing general warnings without enough specificity to give policymakers a chance to take direct action.

Bin Ladin kept plotting, relentlessly, and his followers struck targets overseas and came close in the United States. The immediate backdrop for the threat as the Bush era opened was the *Cole* bombing in October 2000, the al-Qa'ida strike against a US warship during a port visit in Yemen in which seventeen Americans died. The script was familiar: an explosives-laden fiberglass boat approached the port side of the destroyer in Yemen's Aden harbor, while the ship was on a routine refueling stop. The explosion ripped a hole in the side of the ship at the waterline.*

Plots in Yemen in 2000 informed the assessments the following year about where al-Qa'ida might hit next when the Bush team took office. Most officers thought the plotting, which they watched through the blurry lens of incomplete intelligence, related to another overseas attack, like the *Cole* plot or the mas-

---

* The failed attack against the US destroyer *The Sullivans* was a warning before the *Cole*. While the ship was in port in Aden, Yemen, in January 2000, al-Qa'ida attackers attempted to attack the ship with a small vessel laden with explosives. The small boat, however, overloaded with explosives, sank before the attack.

sive bombings at the US embassies in Kenya and Tanzania in 1998. Early in that summer of 2001, the threat information picked up again, so significantly that some officers thought there might be a plot set to correspond to the Fourth of July holiday. Outside the intelligence world, some commentators refer to this kind of information as "chatter," nonspecific references in intercepted communications to shady upcoming events or hazy reports from human informants that lack enough detail to act on. Recalls one CTC manager, "In May or June 2001, threat information was picking up. We thought [a target date of] maybe 4th of July [for an al-Qa'ida attack]. We briefed everybody across government about our concerns."* Those concerns in mid-2001 were only a few months off.

Senior Agency officials, including Director Tenet, repeatedly spoke to White House presidential advisers as part of that briefing barrage in mid-2001. "They [Tenet and his team] understood the threat, they just couldn't convince anybody," remembers one CTC manager from that time. The new presidential team hadn't been seared by attacks on their watch, and the response to the warnings lacked the experience that previous White House officials had brought to the biggest threat stream. The new team wasn't ignoring terrorism, they were just on a learning curve, in the eyes of senior Agency officials.

Some senior CIA executives from that time think the disruption of the Millennium plot raised expectations in Wash-

---

* One former senior official, at the top level of the CIA, had a simple view: "They just won't listen," he remembers thinking. One of those briefers from the relatively small counterterrorism staff at CIA was Jennifer Matthews. Eight years later, in 2009, she would die at the hands of a suicide bomber, killed at a CIA base in Khost, Afghanistan, when an al-Qa'ida plant pretending to be a CIA source entered the Khost compound and detonated a suicide bomb. It was one of the most devastating losses of life the CIA ever experienced.

ington. Many Agency insiders viewed that threat as among the most significant they had ever faced. But they thwarted it, dodging a terrorism bullet with a global effort that was remarkable at that time. The end result, in their view, was that policymakers thought they could handle future threats with the same limited capability. The attitude—"You handled this one, you can handle the next ones the same way"—sidestepped the problem the Agency had faced during the entire decade. If you play defense forever, without bringing the fight to the adversary, you're eventually going to lose one. And they did.

Despite CTC's steps forward, its maturation, its budget, and its leadership, the officers in the al-Qa'ida hunt in the lead-up to 9/11 remember a growing sense of frustration. They saw al-Qa'ida emerging—what Tenet referred to as the threat lights "blinking red" before the attacks. These officers, recollecting the mood in the years before the attacks, speak of quiet desperation interspersed with successes that disrupted other plots but failed to damage al-Qa'ida. One counterterrorism manager during that time characterizes his views today as "deep disappointment." "Shame," he goes on, "would be too strong. We did as much as we could, given the fact that we had limited resources and the US government had other priorities."

3

The Prelude to the Program

All the years of limitations and frustrations during the 1990s and into the new century changed on the day of the attacks. Everything was new. What would have been an unimaginable blue-sky exercise at the White House on September 10 was perfectly acceptable, even too conservative, a day later. As time slips by and a succeeding generation remembers 9/11 as an historical event, it is hard to replicate the tensions, personal motivations, pressures, and the sense of national will that drove CIA officers.

The morning was chaotic. Tenet was at a breakfast in downtown Washington, and other senior officers were scattered. One of the top Agency leaders found himself so caught in the Washington maelstrom that he never made it back to Langley that day. As the reports streamed in on live TV, the reactions at Langley mirrored what the rest of America felt. Some thought there might be as many as 10,000 dead.

Meanwhile, there was reason to believe that the Agency compound might be on the hit list for another plane, and Agency employees surged from the building to the surrounding parking lots. Nobody knew what the rest of the day would bring. Were there five more planes in the air? A hundred? In 1995, an earlier plot conceptualized by Khalid Shaykh Mohammed—and presaging the September 11 attacks—was disrupted in the Philippines before it ever got off the ground. The plot, code-named Bojinka, was stunning in its scope; the plotters aimed to kill the Pope, take down a total of eleven airliners, and crash a plane into CIA headquarters.

Many CTC officers stayed in their seats while the rest of the headquarters compound was evacuated and questions swirled about whether a plane would home in on Langley. Quickly, everyone in the Center knew that the New York, Washington, and Pennsylvania planes held al-Qa'ida plotters. That became clear when CTC officers ran the names through a CIA database and identified them as well-known al-Qa'ida members.

As America sifted through the ashes, al-Qa'ida members celebrated halfway around the world. The diary of one from those days recounts the sense of jubilation they felt:

> As for the inside [inside Afghanistan], happiness was not enough, as soon as the news [of the attacks] came out on the radio, lambs were slaughtered [for feasts], and juice and sweets were distributed for several days, and then, preparations started for the counter attack. News on the radio reflected American threats and preparations, close to a world war, while we were in a state of elation that only God knows.*

---

* Abu Zubaydah diary, volume 6, p. 14.

Back at Langley, as the days progressed and the picture of the attacks slowly came into focus, the long experience of the central core of terrorism believers that Black and Tenet had cultivated gave the Agency a few small advantages. Around the Agency, counterterrorism officers were viewed as true believers, sometimes as outcasts, never part of the mainstream. Now they shifted to the center of the Agency, fueled by the frustrations of the secret battle they had fought for the last decade.

One CIA operations manager who sat above the CTC saw contrast in the more stand-back attitude elsewhere at Langley. "The CTC guys were always very emotional about this stuff," he says, a characterization that many senior CIA officials would say was understated.

They weren't alone. The uncertainty about what al-Qa'ida had in store after 9/11 kept Washington guessing about what was real and what was rumor. On the day of September 11, for example, senior officials remember many false reports of additional attacks, from a widely circulated report of a fire at the Department of State to phantom stories of additional planes in the air. Then, starting a week after 9/11, a series of anthrax-laced letters arrived at various locations.

The first batch of letters appeared at news outlets, with another wave delivered in early October. Over time, the FBI investigation fixed on various American scientific researchers, not al-Qa'ida. The lack of an al-Qa'ida link wasn't clear initially, though, and the anthrax scare immediately sparked a concern that al-Qa'ida had planned this new method as an even more sinister tactic than the airplane strikes.

CIA officers felt more than a professional urgency: they were gripped by a sense of personal responsibility that ran deep. "It's on us," some CIA officers thought as they considered their personal missions and the Agency's central role in the new fight, despite the fact that many government departments and agencies also shifted dramatically to the counterterrorism war. One former official who was at the center of CIA leadership, and of the detention and interrogation program, went further: "They forgave us for the first one. They won't forgive us for the second one." One officer describes deep disappointment that the entire government hadn't mobilized to deal with this emerging threat. "What I felt was near shame," he recalls, "about our lack of focus, mission, purpose, determination. We did not have the warrior ethos to go kill the enemy. The enemy was waging war against us, but we weren't waging war against them." Again and again, officers use different words to contrast these constraints with the post-attack world. As another officer reflected after 9/11, "I felt like the tiger had been set free."

For many, the televised images of jumpers—office workers escaping from the flames of the twin towers by leaping to their deaths rather than facing incineration—was the most searing memory. Several senior CIA officers later talked about these jumpers as a part of the motivation to develop the interrogation process. "Everything had changed [as a result of the attacks]," one remarked. "I wanted to be a part of the solution." Part of his rationale? "People had to choose between burning to death or jumping off buildings. It just completely changed my life." Added one of the operational managers working on the CIA executive corridor at that time, "The planes seemed like a movie. The one image I couldn't shake was the people jumping out of buildings."

Just as personal attitudes drove the Agency to new directions overnight, US government policy also flipped overnight from cautionary to risky aggressiveness. This reversal was clear everywhere after the attacks. Repeatedly, Tenet would look at senior officers and pose a simple question that captured the essence of this aggressive drive, "If there's another attack today, what haven't we done that we will look back on and regret?" This kind of question reflected the tenor of the time: do it today, don't wait, and don't ask permission.

Later, President Bush wrote a note that made its way back to the Counterterrorism Center. That note hung on the wall: "Wanted: Dead or Alive." It was a reference to bin Ladin and captured the no-holds-barred, frontier attitude that permeated operations after 9/11, and it was one of a thousand signals to CIA officers that every element of American life, from the president to everyday citizens, was behind them. Everywhere, CIA officers heard the same sentiments from a cross section of America. Says one of the managers who helped lead the post-9/11 fight, "It was retribution, across society, across politics."

This pressing leadership directive continued down the line to senior operational managers. "The message I got from Cofer [Black, then chief of the Counterterrorism Center], Tenet, and the President was a 180-degree turn," said one officer involved in organizing the initial fight against the Taliban in late 2001. "The mission orders were to find, engage, and kill al-Qa'ida. Very clear, and repeated from every level of the chain of command. There was zero doubt about the mission." Officers who managed the Program talk about a similar commitment to do everything it took to prevent another attack. "The gloves came off," many said, and still say, without regret. Always behind this was that other sentiment: You want to criticize us for not pursuing this target harder, before the attacks. OK. We got it. You won't criticize us again for how aggressive we are.

This rapidly developing war quickly turned out to be a one-of-a-kind intelligence problem, and not just because of the number of deaths or the fact that the attacks occurred inside the United States. This American war, unlike others the Agency participated in, wasn't a conventional Pentagon-managed operation backed by intelligence. Instead, a new age began, an intelligence-driven campaign, with the Agency leading the fight to acquire information from the adversary and then using its own intelligence, was fused with information from other agencies, to dismantle the global al-Qa'ida network. Because intelligence was so critical, CIA officials viewed their agency as uniquely responsible, among all US government agencies, for whether the war succeeded. Meanwhile, their intelligence picture of al-Qa'ida was not well developed. Says a former manager from the CIA's uppermost ranks, "We were on our back foot through at least 2004." They simply didn't know what they didn't know.

President Bush posed a broad variety of questions to CIA director Tenet during the daily morning intelligence briefings in the Oval Office, often with other senior officials in attendance, including Vice President Dick Cheney and National Security Adviser Condoleezza Rice. For past presidents, and earlier for the still-new Bush, those briefings centered on intelligence secrets. In the new war, though, woven into the intelligence briefings were discussions about how the CIA's information would feed directly into tactical counterterror operations, and what the US government should do based on the intelligence the CIA director personally delivered. The discussions were also sometimes more expansive, such as whether the president needed to intercede with foreign leaders on matters related to counterterrorism policy or operations.

The Agency became highly tactical. Tenet might inform the president of the activities of a senior al-Qa'ida plotter while CIA officers put in place the raid to take down that plotter the next day, or the next week. "The President wanted to know everything," says one senior CTC officer.

The sense of the unknown, whether the CIA had any more of the precious commodity of time, was everywhere. One of the most common catchphrases in the intelligence world was always lurking: It's always what you don't know that will kill you. On al-Qa'ida, Agency officials thought they knew precious little. They were reading secret messages from al-Qa'ida, but they had little access to al-Qa'ida players by CIA human informants. "We really didn't have great sources,"* says one of the executive-suite managers who spanned the pre- and post-9/11 eras. "We were in the same boat in August 2002 as we were a year earlier; our sources were too peripheral. We needed to penetrate the inner circle." His judgment matches that of many managers then.

Discussions about detainees weren't a part of those early post-attack months. The CIA hadn't captured any senior al-Qa'ida members—and they wouldn't, until the spring of 2002—and the Agency hadn't yet developed tactical information that would result in captures and force the decision-making about what to do with senior al-Qa'ida prisoners. The lesser captures from the early post-9/11 months were easier to handle; low-level terrorists didn't merit a focused interrogation.

There were also more immediate priorities than thinking about a pie-in-the-sky detainee problem, starting with the CIA–US military partnership with the local militia (the Northern

---

* CIA officers use the word "sources" or "assets" to refer to individuals, typically overseas, who provide information to the Agency. The FBI often uses the word "informants."

Alliance) in Afghanistan and continuing through the escalation in global operations that included partnerships with security services in Asia, the Middle East, Africa, Europe, and Latin America. Everywhere, counterterrorism operations exploded, almost overnight. Within weeks after the attacks, CIA paramilitary teams flew into Afghanistan. This stunning acceleration of the pace of operations, and the stunning audacity of this new world of covert action and partnership with the military, consumed the days. Going into the winter of 2001 and early 2002, the everyday briefings for CIA director Tenet included heavy doses of the paramilitary war, the push against the Taliban, and the takeover of territory that had served as a safe haven for the al-Qa'ida leadership. There was way too much present reality going on to contemplate future "what ifs."

The new operational focus of the Agency, and the magnitude of the decisions surrounding the expansive counterterror campaign, were breathtaking not only in the speed of decision-making but also in the wide scope and newness of the Agency's problems. The CIA teams in Afghanistan had to develop procedures to help with targeting by America's newest weapon, the armed UAVs—drones. Almost immediately, they became part of the US intelligence arsenal. The Agency also needed a method to track its sources quickly so that they could ensure CIA agents weren't caught in bombing raids in this new war zone, especially given the massive airstrikes against Afghan targets every day. (The process that helped the Agency track its informants and keep them from being hit inadvertently in US airstrikes became known as the "magic map" at the Agency, the method the CIA used to maintain an up-to-date registry of the locations of its sources.)

Drone operations alone are a reminder of the vast changes underway. The Agency had only recently started using drones for surveillance. Satellites launched into space could provide images of al-Qa'ida facilities in Afghanistan, but drones had what intelligence professionals call "dwell time": they can remain over a training compound, a car, a residence for an extended period, allowing analysts to study activity there, such as when people gather, what types of vehicles come and go, and whether paramilitary training is taking place.

As the Agency quickly shifted to using armed drones, managers had to develop policies and procedures for everything—from which terrorists rose to a level appropriate for targeting with a drone Hellfire missile to how to limit the loss of civilian life and how low to push authorization for strikes. Drones were one of many areas, later to include detainees and interrogations, where the policy challenges were daunting not only in terms of day-to-day management but also ethically.

Meanwhile, the Agency partnership with military special forces and local partners, the so-called Northern Alliance of anti-Taliban militia members, retook ground more rapidly than they ever could have imagined. The alliance had worked: it had manpower, knowledge of the area, and a will to fight. The CIA thus brought rapid infusions of cash, intelligence, and strategy, along with the lethality of airstrikes. Mundane decisions—where to house a new CIA nerve center in Kabul, for example—came fast and furious, because the capital had fallen.

Americans first set foot in the country in late September, and by later that fall they were in Kabul, setting up headquarters at a hotel. The CIA and the military had complementary skills, with the Agency's history of dealing with some of the Afghans and its flexibility in decision-making on where to move and how to disperse money without huge bureaucratic hurdles. With the military's massive resources, airpower, and special forces' expertise, the only American option for the future would be joint teams, which proved remarkably effective during late 2001. For example, when the CIA was providing money and intelligence to individual Afghan militias then, their special-operations military partners, joining them in the field, might be providing targeting information for strikes by US aircraft. The teams worked well together in the field, and they sometimes bunked with each other in those converted hotel quarters in Kabul.

That military-CIA operational partnership was unheard of before 9/11. One senior Agency official remembers a conversation with a Pentagon four-star general about the emerging cooperation, shortly after the attacks. These would be rough-and-ready operations, Americans on horseback in the no-man's-land of Afghanistan, alongside a ragtag Afghan militia. "What do we do about uniforms?" the CIA official remembers the general saying. "If our men don't wear uniforms, they're not a military. They don't fall under the Geneva Convention," he continued, referring to the international agreement that governs laws of war. They had applied the same standard to al-Qa'ida. "They're not an army, they don't govern territory, they don't wear uniforms, so Geneva didn't apply," said one official, capturing what many thought.

The general's reflections weren't outlandish, they simply reflected how starkly different this new world seemed to every element of Washington's national security apparatus. The transition from a post–Cold War mentality to the new counter-terrorism rules was the largest sea change the US intelligence community had ever faced. And the successes and failures that followed often reflected the fact that this was new territory. Nobody had experience navigating the decisions of the century's first decade.

4

The CIA Revolutionizes

As the Agency dealt with the aftermath of the attacks, the inner workings of the CIA's bureaucracy shifted. After a half-century of chasing the traditional targets of the post–World War II era, especially the Soviets, the Agency now hunted an adversary that had no government sponsor, no clear lines of control or organizational chart, no well-defined capital or geographical center, a hazy chain of command, and equally fuzzy linkages to affiliated groups across the globe.

The breadth and depth of the counterterror war after 9/11 cemented the profound organizational changes at the CIA, some of which had a direct impact on the interrogation program. First was the huge increase in size of the Counterterrorism Center and the massive influx of personnel from other elements across the Agency. As offices were required to transfer personnel to the CTC within days or weeks, the Center's spaces started to expand to new corners of the Langley CIA complex. There was no single suite of office space even close to large enough to house the Counterterrorism Center. A single department within the Center grew larger than any other operational component across the Agency. It wasn't just that the Center dwarfed other operational components; even its unwieldy constituent pieces overshadowed them. Before long, the Agency built trailer-style additions on the Langley compound just to house the overflow. It was all improvised, unplanned, and sometimes haphazard. As some officers said, it was like flying a plane while adjusting its design in mid-air. Mistakes, in retrospect, were almost inevitable. The trade-off was simple: speed in exchange for perfect planning and precision.

One of the Counterterrorism Center's operational leaders from that post-attack time recalls crossing paths with operations officers frequently. "Just get me a job, put me on the team anywhere," he would be asked in the halls, by officers who wanted a transfer to what became, overnight, the operational heart of the CIA. One of the key managers who helped build the Program was just one of many feeling a palpable sense of purpose at Langley. "On Tuesday morning [after September 11]," he recalls, "I said, 'I want in.' On Friday morning, I was there." He remembers dozens of officers transferred with the same speed during the same week.

Some senior officers portray the personnel battles that inevitably resulted as the writhing of an organization that was pivoting between an old mission where the rules were generally established over decades—spy versus spy—and a new mission that some officers viewed as high risk and nontraditional. Others embraced it. One officer who represented this path was Hank Crumpton, a senior officer who had been assigned overseas not long before the attacks. He returned to CIA headquarters to lead the campaign in 2001–2 to partner with the Northern Alliance and roll back the Taliban, which had controlled roughly 90 percent of Afghanistan in mid-2001. Said a former senior official who was involved in the personnel transfers from that time, "Hank reached out. He came with a list. 'I need these people to create this special operations program,' he said. 'Hank came with a list.'" The Counterterrorism Center saw the other side of those birthing pains, with officers unfamiliar with the counterterrorism mission streaming in and some CIA elements, forced to transfer a percentage of their workforce, cherry-picking some of their weaker candidates.

At an institutional level, the massive personnel shifts to the Counterterrorism Center, particularly from the operational side of the Agency, weren't always as smooth as those individual transfers of motivated officers. Some managers were not as enthusiastic as the individuals who volunteered for duty. There were personnel battles during those days. The same senior official who recalls Crumpton's request remembers that "the system had to be undermined to work. One senior officer entered my office yelling that the transfers were undermining operations in Europe." Senior Agency managers led by Tenet and Buzzy Krongard, who as the Agency's executive director managed areas such as the budget and human resources across the CIA, were clearly and unambiguously directing a massive shift in Agency resources, all flowing toward the Counterterrorism Center.

Krongard was a central figure during Tenet's tenure. In early 2001, Tenet tapped him to modernize the CIA's business practices, sometimes against a resistant, tradition-bound bureaucracy with little appetite for the ideas of the outsider Tenet. He had risen rapidly from a staff position on a congressional committee responsible for overseeing US intelligence agencies to the directorship of the CIA, which was not an organization that always respected the chain of command or the ideas of people who didn't fully understand the CIA's culture. If anything, Krongard was even more of an outsider than Tenet in the Agency's closed world, with his history in big-money banking and his lack of experience in government. He was the opposite of warm and fuzzy, but in this secret society, his blunt style, his relationship with Tenet, and his background in the military smoothed his transition. It didn't hurt that he loved the intelligence business, and that he befriended the Agency's senior workforce. They didn't know it, but they needed him more than he ever needed them, by a long shot. Over time, Tenet and Krongard worked to fit in at Langley, and the workforce came to embrace them.

Some shifts reflected a basic bureaucratic bias found in any organization: if I have a choice, some managers might ask themselves, I'll use this opportunity to dump some deadwood personnel. Not all motivations were unreasonable, though. Remembers one senior manager from outside CTC, "People never said, 'Let me send over my top ten percent.'" So many personnel were shifting, and so quickly, that some weaker employees inevitably became part of the mix.

Agency managers were contending with old Agency organizational concepts that were hard to break, as CTC moved from being an Agency outlier to the core of the CIA's business. The Agency's organizational chart includes departments called "area divisions," which are responsible for developing personnel and managing operations related to a specific region. In the decades after World War II, as the Agency developed its institutional culture, these divisions became the heavyweights at headquarters, their spy cases top priorities. The officers didn't chase terrorists; they went after core interest areas from Russians and Chinese to North Koreans, Iranians, and Cubans. In CIA jargon, their countries are known as "hard targets," priorities for America's national security interests but tough areas for recruiting spies.

The Counterterrorism Center didn't pursue traditional hard

targets; terrorism was a phenomenon that came long after the Agency's culture had hardened. For officers who built careers hinged on spotting, assessing, developing, recruiting, and running spies, the counterterrorist targets simply didn't compete as a long-term career option. Counterterrorism was unique, and interesting. But before 9/11, it wasn't a career option; it was a dead end.

The duration of the assignments for the newly transferred officers reflected that institutional resistance to the massive shift underway at the Agency as the organizational aftershocks continued at Langley. Some transferred officers remained tethered to their home offices, with assignments to CTC that were supposed to last only a few months; others had year-long assignments, still short for any bureaucracy trying to plan for the future. Many stayed on, though, energized by the work and its impact, and their capability, unique in the Agency, to tap into CTC's huge resources and newly minted authorities to operate against terrorists with few restraints.

There was an even tougher organizational hurdle, though, that challenged the Center's ability to grow expertise before 9/11. It's the kind of bureaucratic caste system that might seem impenetrable to outsiders even as it is gospel to insiders. In CIA terms, that hurdle can be captured in one obscure term: home-basing. In almost any organization, especially large ones, employees think about career paths and what they might aspire to become over time. But because CTC had always been viewed as a career afterthought, officers there were on "rotation" from other offices, typically area divisions; they were not home-based in CTC, and the Center had relatively few home-based positions. They would eventually return to their home division, to chase hard targets. There just wasn't a level playing field between CTC and Agency heavyweights like Russia House. After 9/11, the number of CIA officers who home-based in CTC grew rapidly.

Meanwhile, another side of the CTC also mushroomed quickly, within weeks: the analytic side, a group of people who assessed what the field operators were collecting and combined it with intelligence from other agencies. CTC's analytic component was a secondary player then in the Directorate of Intelligence, the arm of the Agency that assesses global events and analyzes the intelligence sent in from CIA informants overseas.

Every morning, senior managers from the Agency's analytic offices gathered in the Agency's version of a morning newspaper meeting, discussing what "current intelligence"—the CIA's version of breaking news—would go into the following morning's highly classified intelligence digest for Washington policymakers from the president on down. Before 9/11, the manager from CTC sat on the periphery of the meeting, a backbencher, a clear indicator of the status of terrorism analysis in contrast to issues such as weapons proliferation, Russia, China, or the Middle East.

The head of analysis for the Agency, Winston Wiley, turned that status around immediately after the attacks, in a bureaucratic shift that was more rapid and dramatic than even his own counterterrorism managers anticipated. He had been away from CIA headquarters on the day of the attacks because of transportation bottlenecks in the city. The day before, in one of the many twists of fate from that time, he had told the Agency's deputy director that the time had come for him to retire. On September 11 his plans changed. Wiley told them that he would immediately create a counterterrorism-analysis office with staff that was more than six or seven times the size of the pre-9/11 analytic workforce. "Mock up an office," he directed.

The decision to opt for radical personnel shifts happened almost immediately, and new personnel flowed in. The unprecedented redirection of resources was on, driven by an executive who made the decision that he would rather be criticized for overreacting to the still-emerging crisis than responding too slowly or too timidly. "Easiest decision I ever made," he recalled, fourteen years later. That flood of new talent had a steep learning curve—some had been focused on issues far afield from terrorism, but some excelled in areas as disparate as the former Soviet Union and traditional analyses of foreign weapons systems. For example, some who had studied threats from foreign weapons systems in other areas of the Agency came to CTC and grounded themselves, in months, in the far more informal, sometimes oddball, reporting about al-Qa'ida research into anthrax and more arcane, off-the-shelf agents and poisons, including rotting meat and chemical gases designed to be released in small enclosed areas, such as a subway car. Late one evening not long after the attacks, Wiley faced a question that underscored how jarring the shift was. "When are we going back to the old way?" a subordinate asked. "We're not," came the answer.

Wiley was one of those longtime bureaucrats whose combination of entrepreneurial initiative and deep knowledge of the Agency's corridors allowed him to move up quickly. Like Cofer Black, Wiley didn't mind taking risks, and Tenet rewarded him for doing so. Wiley shifted resources and pushed resistant personnel without hesitation. The willingness to favor boldness over caution proved invaluable, as seen in quick moves to pass information to homeland security and law enforcement authorities that were not traditional partners, such as police departments. In an Agency that pressed its employees to keep secrets, this overnight willingness to share sensitive material with new allies was a massive culture shift. The Agency's leadership sometimes moved without planning out every step, though occasionally that agility proved double-edged.

5

The Problem with Prisoners

During all the policy deliberations under Clinton and into the first stage of the George Bush administration, one unshakeable decision never changed: what do to with al-Qa'ida captives picked up in overseas raids. Under successive administrations, Republican and Democrat, presidents had authorized US intelligence, working with foreign partners overseas, to capture terrorists and transfer them to third countries for prosecution and incarceration. Known as "rendition," the practice of capturing and detaining suspected terrorists and transferring them to another country, often their home country or a location that had a legal case against the detainee, drew international criticism from human rights groups, but it became a core of US counterterrorism policy. Presidents George H. W. Bush and Bill Clinton both authorized the policy; it was a better solution, in the eyes of US intelligence, than either letting a terrorist operate or bringing him (the rendered prisoners were always men) back to the United States for trial when Americans might not have a clear legal case.

A few detainees came to the United States for prosecutions. Most ended up in foreign custody, often with the United States demanding assurances that the prisoner would be treated humanely. Despite the assurances, international critics shared a common view on this policy: the US was handing over prisoners for foreign governments to do the dirty work—harsh questioning—that America couldn't, or wouldn't, do.

The policy of rendition had other problems as well. The CIA didn't always have great insight into what happened once a detainee was sent to his home country. Before the attacks, longstanding CIA policy prohibited officers from participating directly in foreign services' debriefings or interrogations of terrorist prisoners. The CIA passed its own questions for the detainee—questions are called intelligence "requirements" in the spy business—to a foreign service via a local CIA office. That foreign service then "serviced" those requirements, under the pre-9/11 policy, asking the detainee the CIA's questions and passing back the answers in written reports that became formal intelligence disseminated by the CIA to Washington agencies.

That prohibition stemmed from the Agency's early, and checkered, history with interrogations. Agency officers had participated in interrogations during the Vietnam War, and later, in the early 1980s, the Agency developed training programs for foreign security services. They weren't allowed to call this "interrogation" training; that was seen as too sensitive. Instead, they came up with a classically bureaucratic replacement name: Human Resource Exploitation training. Agency activities in Latin America, though, came under scrutiny for human rights violations, and those abuses included the interrogation. In 1986, the Agency ended the training program.

The CIA thus depended on foreign partners to question detainees. Those partners were willing to have the CIA's questions answered partly because the CIA had helped capture them. The Agency also regularly "rendered" prisoners during the pre-9/11 years to their countries of origin. There was no notable political opposition to the renditions; they had continued during the Clinton years, and there was no reason to believe they would stop under the new Bush presidency. "Everybody was happy with it," said one of CTC's top operators from that period.

Those renditions, though, also left CIA officers at arms-length from the terrorists they helped obtain. Officials were not able to access the prisoners because of the old rules prohibiting them from directly participating in debriefings with foreign security services. For the counterterrorism practitioners before 9/11, the reasons for this prohibition were unclear. Few remembered the background for the rules with any certainty, but they operated under the rules: when a foreign service questions a terrorist the United States has rendered, they own the debriefing. The Americans stay out.

This limitation had an upside—managing the risk that CIA officers would somehow become embroiled in human rights allegations or abuses. But it also had a critical downside in its timeliness. In the world of counterterrorism, stopping the next plot is always the first priority, and stopping plots based on stale information is a poor substitute for firsthand access to a detainee. After a detainee's capture, a terror organization knows it has lost one of its members. Plots are postponed but not abandoned; plotters and terror leaders reposition themselves; and terror coordinators and operatives alter communications methods or patterns. Some threat reporting after a terrorist takedown can be extremely time-sensitive. The renditions program, and the rules against direct questioning of terrorists, were not designed for timeliness.

Foreign security services, while thankful for receiving their citizens back home, did not often process US government questions quickly. First, they might have their own questions to ask of a detainee. Second, they might want to filter or adjust what information they passed back to the United States. Another reason was sensitivity; if a detainee revealed information that embarrassed his home country, such as information about fundraising for terrorism within that country, that security service might conceal the information from the Americans. Said one former counterterrorism official, "Some of these prisoners went into a black hole after we rendered them."

The foreign intelligence filter also lessened the effectiveness of the information that flowed in after renditions. One of the reactions among senior CTC officers after 9/11, as they hastily put together war plans for the new al-Qa'ida fight, was that the United States could no longer afford the slowness of working through foreign partners. And as one officer said, "All we knew is what they told us."

This detention issue, when it did come up before the attacks, was purely a conceptual exercise, and a marginal one at that. Renditions were well known across the US government, and they were seen as a perfectly acceptable approach because there simply weren't other alternatives. As one former counterterrorism leader explained, "We asked ourselves what we'd do if we got more than one or two. The issue always seemed bigger than us. We figured people with more resources and experience would handle the problem, mostly the Pentagon."

The Counterterrorism Center's pre-war motto—"Preempt,

Disrupt, Defeat"—included nothing about "imprison." Senior CTC officers in 2017 do not remember ever considering a detention option for the Agency before 9/11. The renditions operations paid off in the rapid decision-making days following the attacks; "Everything was warp speed after," remembers one executive-level manager. But before, this prospect of how to handle a flood of detainees was, as one senior officer described it, a "piss ant issue, sort of like considering flood insurance in Reston [one of the outlying Virginia suburbs]." It wasn't at all within the realm of the pre-9/11 reality. One former senior executive from CTC recounts, "At that time [before the attacks], there was no consideration of any enhanced interrogation. None. It never came up in my time. There were no memos, no meetings."

Across the US government, officials were still focused on terrorism as a law enforcement problem, while the new Bush Administration prepared to take office. Captured terrorists would either be brought to the United States for prosecution or sent to a country that could prosecute. This law enforcement approach extended to bin Ladin. The discussions, says one senior CTC manager who participated in many interagency discussions during this period, centered on "could DoJ [the Department of Justice] put together a criminal case that would result in his conviction. The answer wasn't reassuring."

6

Salt Pit

Afghanistan is a remarkably isolated, hostile environment, from the massive, serrated Hindu Kush Mountains of the north to the blistering hot plains in the south, bordering Pakistan, Iran, and Central Asia. Landlocked and desperately poor, the country has nonetheless been a historical crossroads in South Asia, with the march of Alexander the Great and, centuries later, the invasion of the vaunted Soviet Red Army in 1979.

That Soviet invasion turned Afghanistan from a land of a civil war on the periphery of American policy to the center of a global ideological conflict between the Soviet empire and America's policy to contain the spread of Soviet-style Communism. When the Soviets invaded to prop up their Communist ally in Kabul, the Americans responded by aiding rebel groups who became known as the mujahideen. It wasn't until fifteen years later that the equation began to shift again, as a new force, the conservative religious movement known as the Taliban, swept from its southern heartland north. Some of the same warlords the Americans had supported to blunt the Soviet Army fought the Taliban, but by the late 1990s they were losing ground.

The Taliban was poised to tighten its grip through mid-2001. Fighting in the north marked what seemed then to be the final phase of the Taliban's takeover of all Afghanistan, with some of the last anti-Taliban holdouts favoring the fundamentalist militia. The Soviets were gone, and the Americans, too, had lost interest in Afghanistan after the last Soviet troops withdrew. With the country's economy in shambles and diplomatic interest and aid diminished, the Taliban as a result pushed far outside its base near the southern border with Pakistan and into ethnically diverse provinces far north.

The Taliban's gains, and Afghan militias' vicious and persistent resistance to the Soviet invasion, left many in Washington concerned about whether America's rapid entry into the country after 9/11 would turn into a quagmire. Those well-founded concerns, though, turned out to be dramatically incorrect, at least in the short-term. As rapid as the CIA's post-9/11 revolution was in Washington, it wasn't as rapid as the early successes in this distant battlefield against the Taliban. CIA field operators and US military special forces, in partnership with the Northern Alliance— the Afghan fighters in the north of the country who had battled the Taliban before 9/11—made major strides within weeks.

During the 1980s, the Soviet Red Army had struggled against the Afghan resistance. Now, the Northern Alliance and its American allies turned back the Taliban tide, which had spread across more than three-quarters of the country. With air support, money, equipment, and the combination of local Afghan fighters and American intelligence and special operators, the United States rolled up territorial gains against the Taliban faster than even a naïve optimist could have anticipated. The years-long struggle of the Soviet Army, with its massive resources and scorched-earth tactics, led to an anticipation after 9/11 that an American intervention might face equally long odds. Some used the word "quagmire" shortly after the US invasion of Afghanistan, judging that the Americans would be bled dry just as the Soviets had been. But the partnership with the Northern Alliance proved crucial, and the Taliban lost its southern stronghold of Kandahar just three months after the 9/11 attacks, marking a breathtaking transition from a Taliban that had threatened to take over the entire country in September.

The surprising, unanticipated successes against the Taliban during those initial weeks and months left the Agency with its first decision, what to do with detainees. Said one of the senior Agency operators working in Afghanistan, remembering the waves of prisoners: "We were picking people up right and left. . . . The military couldn't take them. So we built Salt Pit. We could have turned them over to the Afghans, but the al-Qa'ida guys would pay the guards and get them released. We built our own. But it turned out half-assed." Not for long.

In those early days of the new war, just months into a conflict no one anticipated or planned for, no officer remembers having clear foresight about the implications of housing the first detainees in Afghanistan. The Agency and its Afghan partners were capturing prisoners in late 2001 who weren't senior al-Qa'ida players; they were lower-level battlefield captures from the Taliban. They were mass groupings of prisoners rolled up during the rapid military operations and held in Afghan detention centers, who weren't in isolated, off-the-grid locations that would allow for long-term, secret interrogations. A few of them were worth detaining and interrogating for their intelligence value—for what they knew about the war, the Taliban, and the fleeing al-Qa'ida members who would make their way across the forbidding Afghan frontier, and the Tora Bora mountain range, and into neighboring Pakistan. The outlines of the first CIA choices in the emerging world of detainee intelligence were developing. What do you do with a prisoner who has important, maybe critical, knowledge about the adversary?

The answer for an Agency that prided itself on its agility? Hold them in Agency facilities. That is to say create an in-house detention center, in a ramshackle existing building, as a bureaucratic branch grafted onto the CIA field element in Afghanistan that was already saddled with too many other responsibilities, including the ongoing war. That ad hoc detention site was a building attached to an older structure—out of place, without any connection to the purpose or design of the original structure. It was an organizational appendage.

"We really didn't know what we were doing," says one senior operations officer familiar with the CIA's early activities in Afghanistan.

The creation of the prison was a back-of-the-envelope operation in design, staffing, and oversight to meet the immediate requirement. In reality, there was no real infrastructure the Agency could build that quickly, and so they were forced to settle on a basic structure. A few Agency officers, including an administration officer who would help with the logistics of the setup, sat down and decided how to build everything. The end result was rough: there was no central heat, no air conditioning, no set standards for medical oversight for prisoners; there weren't policies and procedures to run the facility, and there wasn't a lot of headquarters regulation. There was also weak record keeping. The focus was on maintaining a high operational tempo in the field, with the emphasis on action. "There was inaccurate documentation on prisoner transfers," said one manager from that period.

Without focused planning for the detainee mission, the Agency had its first turning point in the slew of decisions that eventually resulted in what would become the full-fledged Program, the informal term used for the legally authorized detention and interrogation of CIA prisoners at Agency prisons using Department of Justice–authorized interrogation techniques. First, as with any Agency operation, this new prison enterprise needed its own name. Even that seemed rough, a reflection of the primitive facility the Agency used. Two words captured it all: Salt Pit.

The name "Salt Pit" was what the Agency called a cryptonym, a common practice of providing secret names to people, programs, facilities—anything the Agency wanted to obscure in its electronic communications to maintain security. The facility had been referred to by some as the Afghan DetFac (Detention Facility) but it was, in the future, always referred to by its new code name. One officer involved in oversight of that facility remembers thinking that the cryptonym sounded too grim and indicated to Tenet that it would be changed. "Keep it," he remembers Tenet saying, so they did.

When it came to "the Pit," as it was sometimes referred to, all those characteristics that marked the Agency's rapid changes after 9/11 applied to this new problem of housing detainees, particularly the trade-off between risk, speed, and cautious deliberation about a new mission. Agency managers didn't, or couldn't, spend the time developing policies and procedures that might have prevented mistakes.

One field operations officer who visited Salt Pit in 2003 reflected on what had traditionally been the agency's espionage mission. "This was weird. This was not what we did. We stood behind one-way glass. There were these little interrogation rooms. You'd hear loud music. And then they brought a detainee in for questioning. It was jarring. Not interrogation techniques like we had later, but harsh verbal interrogation. The subject was buck naked. And I thought, wow, are we really doing this?" This officer's recollection, and the blunt impact of the CIA's rapid transition into a paramilitary organization that detained and interrogated prisoners, mirrored what officers across the Agency felt. In this case, the officer had been involved in counterterrorism operations before the war. The contrast could not have been more stark. This wasn't classic espionage. This was a prison.

In one of the most chilling moments that defined the CIA's short history of prisoner detentions, that roughshod approach resulted in a critical mistake. The prisoner: Gul Rahman, a name that still haunts every official from that era of counterterrorism operations and Afghanistan. He wasn't a high-profile al-Qa'ida capture; instead, he was a foot soldier fighting for one of the many warlords and militias that remained in Afghanistan after building power bases during the anti-Soviet war. Nonetheless, the Agency thought he might be able to offer valuable intelligence.

Captured in Afghanistan in late October 2002, prior to the CIA's implementing the DoJ-sanctioned Program, Rahman was held in a prison cell, under the supervision of the CIA. Several weeks later, in late November, he was dead. The Senate report that later excoriated the CIA for the Program named him as the only detainee who had died in an interrogation facility, though Salt Pit was far different from the formal Program, which started outside Afghanistan with the first DoJ documentation, in August 2002. The Senate report says Rahman was subjected to " '48 hours of sleep deprivation, auditory overload, total darkness, isolation, a cold shower, and rough treatment'." One night in November 2002 he was "shackled to the wall of his cell," wearing only a sweatshirt and naked from the waist down. He was found dead—likely of hypothermia—the next day, on the bare concrete floor. Other factors in his death included "dehydration, lack of food, and immobility due to 'short chaining.'" The conditions were rough: in a facility with twenty cells, he was held in one of the stand-alone "concrete boxes," according to a CIA after-action report. Four of those cells, including Gul Rahman's, were designed especially for sleep deprivation.

Rahman's death stemmed from many oversights, and it remains one of the few areas former officers point to as a serious, inexcusable mistake during the era of detention and interrogation. For one, the Salt Pit facility, on the periphery for CIA officers focused on the Taliban fight, lacked experienced personnel. The Agency initially assigned young case officers—field officers—to manage a facility that they had no training to run. Field operations were the plum assignments for these officers, not prison management. The CIA office in Kabul, not far from Salt Pit, had some oversight responsibility for the facility, but that office had a wide variety of missions at the time, and no knowledge of how to manage a detainee program. Oversight from the Kabul home-base for Salt Pit was not well defined, and Gul Rahman was held in a facility that was not staffed entirely by CIA officers or contractors.*

Like many turning points in the Agency's years of detaining prisoners, clear leadership direction after Rahman's death drove

---

* CIA officers refer to personnel hired from private companies as "contractors," or contract employees; they do not have the same responsibilities and authorities as government staff personnel. CIA managers are supposed to hire contractors for roles that are beyond the standard jobs held by operators, analysts, and support personnel. For example, CIA operators might be responsible for handling informants inside the al-Qa'ida organization; contractors with specialized technical skills might be hired to develop and build specialized communications gear for the operations officer to maintain contact with the informant.

the Agency to make changes in policies and procedures. The Center's management chain had a few key figures on the organization diagram: there was the director and deputy director of CTC at the top, with chief of analysis and a chief of operations (effectively the field manager of CTC's global counterterrorism fight) directly below.

The operations chief at that time, a tough, legendary CIA field operator who later became the Center's director, reacted swiftly and decisively in the wake of the Salt Pit death in 2002. His legend wasn't built on charm or charisma; he commanded, and demanded, absolute attention to detail, every day. He read everything and expected subordinates to have the same attention to every report from the field, every operation, and every mistake. When he questioned subordinates, he was brutal. But he had an attribute that was hard to beat: an unforgiving thirst for the al-Qa'ida hunt. He came in seven days a week to oversee that hunt and drove CTC officers relentlessly to match his passion. His oversight was clear: field sites were managed by the Special Missions Department in CTC, a unique arm in the Center that had the unusual responsibility not of managing standard CIA offices overseas but instead of overseeing the newly emerging prison network. One senior official who served at black sites remembers, "There was a direct line to the CTC Front Office, especially to [the senior operations officer]." He drove the policy on assigning only senior officers as facility managers and quickly cleared up questions about the chain of command for the facilities.

As a result, lines of command shifted, to ensure clearer oversight of detention operations. Because the site was in Afghanistan, the CIA headquarters entity responsible for overseeing that part of the world also took over responsibility for Salt Pit later in 2002. A CIA office that traditionally was responsible for running secret agents now also had responsibility to help run a war, and that included managing a prison. The result was neglect: not enough attention to the strict rules that the Agency needed, and not even the knowledge that they had to develop strict rules. This lack of persistent, focused, senior-level attention to the management of detainees changed, as CTC streamlined the loose and disparate detention policies at the Agency. After Rahman's death, and on orders from the director of CTC, the Center would run prisons; there would be no questions about who would be in charge, and there would be a dedicated entity at the Agency that would have detention authority and responsibility as its primary mission. The week the clarification in the chain of command for Salt Pit went out, headquarters sent officers to survey the site and found it lacked heat, blankets, and training.

Rules for onsite management changed to ensure that relatively junior officers wouldn't have to run a detention facility. Initially, with prison management as an afterthought, the original officer assigned to run Salt Pit was untrained and inexperienced in dealing with detainees. Henceforth, every officer in charge of every CIA detention facility would be an officer from the Agency's Senior Intelligence Service, the highest-ranking Agency employees at Langley. This was the Agency's equivalent of flag-rank officers in the military, a clear sign that they knew they had to adjust detention practices quickly, and unambiguously.

More shifts followed. Communications practices between headquarters and the field, for example, strengthened, along with the expertise and the care and consideration that come from mistakes and accidents—a death, in this case. Medics hadn't had specific guidance, or a requirement, to attend to detainees. They soon had instructions.

The loosely managed Salt Pit detention facility resulted

partly from the way the Agency trains its officers to think. Be agile. Do whatever it takes to accomplish the mission. We're the US government agency that does the dirty stuff nobody else wants to do, Agency operatives thought. "Nobody else was stepping up," said one former top official, reflecting on the CIA's new detainee mission. As the Agency headed toward the Program decision, that tone persisted. "Just the atmospherics of it all weren't surprising," remembers one former senior manager. "We had already been told that directed action against al-Qa'ida [e.g., lethal military operations] was on the table. So this [the interrogations] didn't surprise me."

In addition to facing the reality of Gul Rahman's death, many senior officers also had another, more mundane reaction to the interrogation mission that no other element of government wanted. Many had seen, or at least had friends who had seen, the impact of after-action reports on covert actions in years past. The Iran-Contra scandal of the 1980s, led by a White House official but touching Agency officers, was a classic example of CIA officers caught in a nasty overseas operation that turned sour. During President Reagan's second term in office, he made the stunning public announcement—as many CIA personnel watched on live TV—that US officials had bypassed a congressional ban on aiding Nicaraguan Contra guerrillas fighting the Soviet-backed revolutionary government there. The pipeline of support was as complicated as it was bizarre: Iran wanted US weapons, such as antitank missiles, and the United States shipped those weapons through a deal with Israel. The US then used the proceeds from the weapons sales to support Contra rebels in Nicaragua. It was as illegal as it was novel.

Of more immediate interest to CIA officers were the efforts to support anti-Communist guerrillas in Latin America, and the allegations that some of those operations involved support for CIA contacts who were human rights abusers. The CIA fired two officers and disciplined others for their involvement in the Iran-Contra affair, one of several insurgencies in which the CIA had become entangled. The Agency is a small organization; the memories of those years, and the ugly disputes about whether CIA operators were dirty, remained prominent reminders, after 9/11, of the perils of high-risk covert actions.

Prominent too were the unaccounted-for Stinger antiaircraft missiles in the hands of the Afghan mujahedeen, the shoulder-fired surface-to-air missiles that had proven viciously effective against Soviet airpower. The US government spent years trying to buy back the weapons, fearful that the same missiles that took down Soviet aircraft would be used against civilian airliners. Even the most successful covert actions are never entirely clean.

The CIA's cadre of overseas operatives took one crucial lesson from earlier operations and the recriminations that followed much later: when you get involved in something potentially controversial, write it down. Get "paper," documentation that shows everything you do, so that when you're later questioned—or accused of wrongdoing or even criminal conduct—there's a clear trail of what you did, why you did it, and who knew.

One of the central players in the Program had spent a long career focused on Latin America before he shifted to the counterterrorism world. "I remembered the covert action days," he said later, referring to the clandestine operations the CIA ran to counter Soviet influence in Latin America. "They left us holding the bag." He was one of many CIA officials who insisted on legal documentation at every step of the way during the evolution of the Program. The questions about potential blowback from controversial covert action programs were sometimes trumped, in 2002, by the across-the-board, consensus support for an all-out campaign against al-Qa'ida that seemed to reach every corner of America. In the early post-attack era, documentation could be lagging, or sloppy, not only because of the imperative of speed but also because the country seemed so unified in support for the Agency to do anything it took on.

Officers who served at this time and as the formal Program developed note feeling a strong sense of national unity during the first year after the 9/11 attacks, before the Iraq war. One of the architects of the legendary paramilitary push that led to the Taliban's striking retreat after 9/11 recounts a meeting with the Northern Alliance in the spring of 2002, when several operations officers met their Northern Alliance counterparts north of Kabul. Among the trees and beside a stream, they enjoyed a lunch, knowing the advance against the Taliban would reverse the years of relentless Taliban rule that had gripped the country before US advisers appeared in the fall of 2001. One of the Americans present remarked on the emotions from both sides, and the pride in the partnership that had produced such success. The Afghans appeared with spectacular carpets, and the conversation became a quiet celebration.

During that lunch, though, the war wasn't the focus of the conversation; instead, it was a manifestation of the value the Afghans perceived in the American teamwork, and what the Americans meant not only for the Northern Alliance but for a country that had been torn by so many years of civil war. It was those kinds of sentiments, similar to the support CIA felt in America at that time, that led CIA officials to believe the partnership at home was tighter than it proved to be. The Program was born of a short-lived, closely woven alliance among typically fractious Washington power players.

Salt Pit wasn't part of any formal network of prisons run under legal guidance provided by the Department of Justice. But it did offer critical lessons about the risks of running a more formal program for al-Qa'ida prisoners. The Agency was learning about this new detention mission. Now all that awaited was the challenge of what to do with the first senior al-Qa'ida prisoner.

7

The First Program Prisoner

Through the spring of 2002, questions about how to grow the new global counterterrorism campaign quickly flowed into Langley. America was still on edge about the next possible attack when another critical decision had to be made. Forget about the captives in Afghanistan who ended up at Salt Pit, low-level detainees who wouldn't know about the next plot. What happens if you net a real al-Qa'ida leader, somebody high up the chain? What do you do then?

In the business of intelligence, there are a few basic ways to acquire knowledge about an adversary. One is sources, the human informants who infiltrate governments and terror groups at the behest of intelligence services. The second is wires, the interception of an adversary's communications—phone calls, emails, text messages, anything that involves electronic transmissions. Getting inside the heart of an adversary by either of those means is elusive; intercepted communications are typically fragmentary, and they do not often offer insights into plans and intentions, the ultimate goal for any intelligence collection.

Top-tier al-Qa'ida players could help the Agency understand not only what the group thought, who low-level operatives were, and how the organization functioned, but also how it was reconstituting after its leaders suddenly fled Afghanistan in the chaos of the post-9/11 war. One of the first prisoners of this kind turned out to be pivotal. His true name was Zayn al-Abidin Muhammad Husayn; he was called Abu Zubaydah. Staying in touch with al-Qa'ida's far-flung operations, in Pakistan and outside, required frequent communication with an informal network of al-Qa'ida supporters. Abu Zubaydah maintained those lines of communication the same way an average citizen would in the early days of 2002: he was communicating to the al-Qa'ida network that was reeling from the US invasion, and US intelligence agencies knew it.

In early 2002, Abu Zubaydah's profile was raised partly because there was a sense that the CIA was closing in on him. He had been a prominent intelligence target for the US intelligence community generally and the CIA in particular since 2000, due to his role and his personality. He was what counterterrorism specialists call a terrorist "facilitator"; he made things happen for the group, serving as an intermediary, arranging travel and helping to manage operations generally. This role forced him to communicate more than many senior al-Qa'ida members whose roles might have focused more narrowly on managing specific terror operations rather than reaching across a broad network of contacts. He also proved to be a hands-on manager, raising his profile and his vulnerability.

Steadily, relentlessly, the CIA began circling Zubaydah. The scent grew more acute as he became a constant feature in the nightly al-Qa'ida briefings for Tenet, with the focus on identifying his location with enough accuracy to mount a raid or a series of raids. Finally, in March 2002, working with a friendly security service, the Agency decided to go after him. The briefings to Tenet included minute detail of how the CIA operators who were tracking him gained bits and pieces of Zubaydah's communications trail.

As the CIA closed in, Abu Zubaydah sensed the pursuit. In diaries captured later, he refers repeatedly to his concerns about the persistent hunt for him. He knew his days as a free man were numbered:

> It has been a while since the news papers and Magazines . . . keep publishing my name from time to time (complete) or the last name which is the family's original last name. Lately, about a week ago, my name was mentioned by a Washington Radio Station as the person in Charge of Communications and Foreign Affairs for Bin LadenBin Ladin . . . ? My security situation became worse. [~~I don't know who gave them these wrong information; there is no relation between us and Bin LadenBin Ladin except Brotherhood in God~~]." [2000]*

> . . .

> "The Pakistani newspapers are chasing me. The matter is now new, as for five years it has been attempting to connect me to anything, and the matter is growing bigger, until they lately said that I am the heir of Bin Ladin for the leadership of Al-Qa'ida Organization. I hope they know that I am not even a member of Al-Qa'ida, so how can I become their leader. Any-

---

* Year 2000, volume 5, page 16. The strikethroughs appear in Abu Zubaydah's original diary, but translators report that the words remain legible.

way, these matters are not important to me; however, its effects on the security situation makes the matter worse, and I need to be more cautious." [2/4/2002]

. . .

"We have left (Lahore, my group and I, and after a brief separation) we met in ~~Lahore~~ Faisal Abad, in a suitable, big house, but it does not lack security gaps." [3/20/2002]

The raid that captured Zubaydah was a high-risk operation, and not just because of the chances of a shootout. The bigger problem was the gamble: according to one manager who worked on the operation, some experts estimated the chances of a successful raid at only 20 to 50 percent. There was a highly uncertain nature of "locational" intelligence designed to trap terrorists half a world away, and a huge premium on picking the right risks to bet on when you could never be entirely certain that the intelligence was accurate or timely. You might know where a terrorist was yesterday, but how about today or tomorrow?

Still, delaying a raid also carried a downside. A change in Zubaydah's location could be crippling, at least temporarily. The CIA might have to spend months, or longer, re-creating an intelligence picture clear enough to even consider another capture operation. That balance—the risk of the raid versus the risk of the target's flight—featured often in CIA operations during those years. Abu Zubaydah was an operator. One wrong raid and not only would he move; he would almost certainly go silent. It was a one-shot deal, over in a single night.

Behind the hunt for this one al-Qa'ida member was the growing sense among CIA executives that they might be closing

in on their first senior al-Qa'ida captive of any sort. That possibility resulted in a ready acceptance of risk from the Agency's
executive corridor—known as "the Seventh Floor" at the CIA—
and created space for innovative operations with big downsides,
an environment as pervasive in the Abu Zubaydah hunt as it was
soon afterward in the establishment and growth of the Program.
It wasn't so much that senior Agency officials either demanded
harsh measures or prodded counterterrorist specialists to come
up with a plan. That didn't happen. The tone was instead a complex web of emotions, some external and some internal, that
drove the "gloves-off" mentality underpinning the Program.

That tone, however, wasn't the only decision-making driver.
Abu Zubaydah's extensive background with extremists, and
particularly his involvement in al-Qa'ida training facilities, also
motivated the human hunters at the CIA. In the 1990s al-Qa'ida
had become a magnet for jihadi trainees from around the world.
Abu Zubaydah helped oversee one of its main training facilities, the Khaldan Camp, so his potential knowledge of recruits
could help the Agency piece together the maze of conspiracies
directed against the West. Like many detainees, Abu Zubaydah
wasn't just important because he might know of current plotting. His knowledge of even tiny bits and pieces of al-Qa'ida's
previous activities, from the code names of trainees to how the
group created documentation for its members, was critical to the
intelligence.

His capture was messy. It happened in Faisalabad, site of the
final entries in Abu Zubaydah's diary. The raid teams, a combination of Americans and Pakistanis, hit several locations. And
they hit pay dirt: Abu Zubaydah was at one of the al-Qa'ida safe
houses, where members stayed or passed through. He didn't
go down without a fight, and an exchange of gunfire left him

injured, particularly in one leg, with a serious wound in the thigh. He received immediate medical attention in Pakistan, but some CIA officers even today believe, not unreasonably, that Abu Zubaydah would have died without the medical treatment the Agency flew in. His injuries were severe. Abu Zubaydah himself later acknowledged that he knew how much American assistance had meant to him. During one conversation, he tapped his leg. "Look," a CIA officer remembers him saying in a conversation, "I'm a prisoner, you could have done anything, and you kept me alive. You didn't take my leg. It would have been a lot easier just to amputate my leg."

He went on to contrast the treatment he received at the hands of his captors to the treatment he would have received at the hands of his fellow al-Qa'ida members, whom he and other al-Qa'ida captives referred to as "the brothers." "In our circles," he said, "they would have cut my leg off. But you people spent time and money to save my leg." He was appreciative—but it didn't matter. He was still in the hands of his adversary. His appreciation didn't limit his will to resist, and it didn't diminish his hatred of his captors.

Good medical care was paramount, and even in the huge bureaucracies of the US government, personal relationships counted. The Agency's executive director, Buzzy Krongard, had connections with physicians that he used to recruit for a rapid trip to Abu Zubaydah's bedside. It was a classic ad hoc CIA move, elegant in its simplicity and speedy execution and without the trappings of bureaucracy, which CIA operators felt compelled to avoid, particularly in those risk-seeking times. As a measure of the speed with which the Agency sent out the new team, they couldn't cover every angle, not that fast. The physician who inserted a catheter later told a colleague he hadn't performed the procedure since medical school.

The medical treatment for Abu Zubaydah went beyond an interest in saving his life. Even then, the Agency wasn't considering aggressive interrogations. Some officers, though, were concerned that if he died, they would not only lose a debriefing opportunity; somebody, especially in the conspiracy-driven world of the Middle East and South Asia, would figure out a way to claim that the CIA killed him.

The questioning started soon, but not right away. Abu Zubaydah's first interrogators were delayed for several weeks after his capture because of his perilous medical condition. And there was another immediate problem: if the Agency felt they were going to hold him long-term—and they had no idea how long—where would he go, assuming it couldn't be a detention facility in the United States? There was no facility that fit the need for housing senior al-Qua'ida prisoners, and nobody had a pat answer for what to do with what became known as HVDs (High Value Detainees).

Before the Agency settled on the first detention site, random proposals about how to find isolated locations included a remote island or a ship—maybe a leased cruise liner—that would simply remain in international waters, never entering port with prisoners aboard. Some were even more farfetched. In the classic Agency tradition of agility and creativity, someone suggested finding an abandoned oil platform, or leasing an existing one. It would be easy to secure and outside US territory, where legal questions about the rights of prisoners on US soil were less clear.

Officers who wanted to help threw out a few ideas that were almost humorous, in retrospect. A CIA office in Africa suggested an island surrounded by crocodiles. This certainly didn't take into account the fact that the Agency would want to interrogate the prisoners, not simply drop them at an isolated location from which they couldn't escape. Another idea, going back to the Contra era in Latin America: the Swan Islands. A tiny, isolated group of islands off the coast of Honduras, these had been discovered by Columbus but were uninhabited apart from a small Honduran military garrison. The idea was shot down, partly, remembers one Program manager, because of concerns that the location would leak. That wasn't the only dead-end proposal: Defense Secretary Donald Rumsfeld also suggested a US ship.

In another surprising proposal that never went far, some raised an Asian country as an option for prisoners, with the rationale that local officials would have broad and deep expertise on detention. This idea was soon put to rest by a senior State Department official. "Interesting," was the response. "But we can't give these guys this leverage. We can't give them a chance to put us over a barrel." Like some of the other proposals, the Asian option wilted quickly. The Agency was agile but the ideas weren't always feasible, or even debatable. Some Agency officials who attended rump sessions that sometimes followed broader counterterrorism meetings remember talk of using truth serums.

Because of the unplanned nature of Abu Zubaydah's capture, that first facility was makeshift. In mid-2002, there wasn't time to design and build a dedicated site. Nor would the CIA have had the expertise to come up with a design. They needed to settle on a ready-built site that they could alter quickly.

During that frenetic period, some Agency officials sat in a room looking at a map, trying to think through what countries might work. In addition to the logistical requirements and political realities, there was also a bureaucratic factor. Most of the Agency's operational management was broken down into "Area Divisions," groups that were responsible for specific regions of the world, such as Africa or East Asia. Some division managers were seen as difficult to work with. On the basis of a quick review of some of the more difficult senior managers in the operations directorate, one participant remembers, some of these regions were taken off the list of potential target spots at the start. Others were off the table quickly because Agency officers weren't confident that leaders in those countries could keep a secret, at least not for long.

As the CIA shifted toward the detention and interrogation business in mid-2002, the CTC's structure evolved to accommodate the new mission. There had long been a group in place—aptly named "Renditions Group"—within CTC to manage the renditions that had been so key since the 1990s. RG, as it was known, was responsible for transporting terrorists from their point of capture or from the custody of a third country to the country where they would be detained long-term. Many of these detainees were wanted in their home countries for terrorist acts or other violations. The United States did not have the legal "paper" to charge them with crimes based on US federal law, but releasing them would leave a known terrorist on the streets. The clearest solution for many detainees would be to send them home to countries that had their own legal cases against them.

Renditions Group was key to the process of identifying locations for proposed detention facilities. This identification process went through a number of stages. First, the Group's managers met with the area divisions, those headquarters units responsible for overseas operations and broken down geographically, with units responsible for regions such as Africa, Latin America, and the Middle East. The Area Divisions oversee the CIA offices in the countries of those regions; CTC managers therefore worked through these divisions as the first step to contacting the CIA's overseas offices to determine which might be appropriate for hosting what became the black site network.

The Area Divisions, working with CTC, then sought the input of chiefs of station (COS)—the CIA officers managing CIA offices overseas—about the appropriateness of a particular country and the COS's relationship with that country's security service. If the answers were positive, Renditions Group staff traveled to the location to meet with liaison security services and determine what they were willing to provide. In one of several steps the CIA took to ensure these potential host countries understood the risk of hosting a black site, these contacts included discussions about which other government officials required briefings on the potential site, and how to seek approval of the head of state. Those risks were predictable in an intelligence world where few secrets remained secrets for long: exposure to other elements of the local government that might be hostile to the presence of CIA sites; attacks and legal action by human rights groups that might already be pursuing potential hosts for these sites; and diplomatic retaliation by other countries that might see these black sites as violations of regional legal, diplomatic, or human rights norms.

After these preliminary steps, Renditions Group then began the intensive survey process. This evolved over time, but surveys initially included assessments of transportation, food, medical treatment, and seclusion. Logistics might seem mundane today, in light of the interrogations that happened at those facilities, but it was key to site selection then. Even at a secure facility, a long drive from the airport might be too much. In some cases, a downtown facility in a major city was preferable.

During this time, the group's name changed, not for the last time. Renditions Group became Renditions and Detention Group in mid-2002, or RDG. They had a new mission, shifting from transferring prisoners around the globe to actually holding them at CIA sites.

CTC was also evolving in other ways. By the spring of 2002 it was clear that the paramilitary phase of counterterrorism—the post-9/11 fight in Afghanistan to oust the Taliban and al-Qa'ida—was closing, and the less military, more intelligence-driven global campaign was gaining momentum. "Rather than gaining ground and pursuing fighters in Afghanistan," one senior manager remembers, "we were transitioning to finding terrorists around the world, one at a time." Continuing the Center's long history of placing operators alongside managers, CTC now integrated management of its units, often with operations chiefs and analytic supervisors co-managing integrated analytic-operational units. It was unique, but it wasn't driven by pure management theory. Agency managers started to see more terror plots generated by groups affiliated to al-Qa'ida but operating outside Afghanistan, and they thought they needed closer partnership between analysts studying the detailed movements of al-Qa'ida terrorists and the operators designing plans to capture them.

In the weeks and months after the Abu Zubaydah capture, cable exchanges between headquarters and CIA field offices included requests that station chiefs ask their interlocutors in foreign security agencies whether that country would consider hosting a detention facility. The station chiefs responded, and one friendly country ended up at the top of the heap for the first facility. After all the back-and-forth, the small group determining where to set up that first facility boiled down the requirements. One official from that time remembers a phrase they came up with for the kinds of countries that would fit their parameters: "countries long on order and short on law." Quickly, the Agency settled on a location, and al-Qa'ida's first detainee would soon have a home. The CIA code-named it "Catseye."

The selection and development of the first location for Abu

Zubaydah stemmed from the drive for speed, the old Agency can-do mindset that was even more prominent in crisis. The country was not put forth by any senior CTC officer; it was proposed from below, as more junior CTC officers were canvassing overseas offices for ideas about where to send the first prisoner.

The early ramshackle facilities had just a few cells—one senior officer referred to the initial detention facility as the "chicken coop"—and few amenities. Catseye combined characteristics that made it a solid choice for this new detention program. First, it was isolated, private, and arranged through a trusted foreign intermediary who wouldn't ask too many questions. There wasn't just a professional relationship with this intermediary: it was an agreement based on trust, and relying on the personal connections with CIA officials that this single intermediary could offer.

CIA partners offered to turn over, at least temporarily, that remote facility, partly because its isolated location moderated security risks that outweighed the logistical problems of supporting the interrogation teams. Local partners helped protect the facility and ensured that the perimeter, and the facility itself, were closely guarded. And the facility had the added benefit of being immediately available. The CIA's first black site was underway.

Catseye wasn't a facility that met US prison standards. Inside the loaned building, the CIA constructed a room within a room, with bars and a few areas where they could "contain" prisoners outside the cell. This was a headquarters-managed effort from the start. In an unusual move, the local CIA chief received a request to stay away. The Program was to be managed by a group independent of local CIA field managers who were more experienced with traditional intelligence programs, such as running clandestine agents. The senior field professionals were CIA employees but they were not subordinate to a standard CIA chain of command that typically would have tied them to the local CIA station. They reported directly home, bypassing the CIA chain of command in the field and talking directly back to Langley.

That first step to Catseye led the Agency to basic questions about why they would hold prisoners in the first place. Aside from their own detention facilities, other options didn't seem even close to defensible. Boiled down to a few choices, the CIA's decisions about what to do with high-level captives were:

- release them;
- hold them indefinitely in CIA custody;
- hand them over to another government or security service, either where they were captured or elsewhere—typically to their home country; or
- imprison them, either as long-term military detainees with an undetermined status or as prisoners bound for prosecution in US courts.

Each option had pitfalls. Releasing them could result in a loss of intelligence and a sustained risk. Some percentage of detainees—30 percent? 70 percent?—would return to the battle-field. And who would ever consider releasing one of the architects of the *Cole* bombing? Or individuals who had been involved in plotting and supporting the 9/11 attacks?

Handing senior al-Qa'ida members over to other security services, even friendly services, also had substantial downsides, particularly for exploiting the detainees' intelligence value. As the interrogation program matured, CIA officers came to value access to detainees that was unfiltered and rapid, with no intermediary who could weed out questions, alter them, or otherwise manipulate an interview process that might be driven by highly specific interests. Further, an unfiltered process imme-diately eliminated questions about whether an intermediary security service might alter a detainee's responses when pass-ing them back to the Agency. If the detainee revealed something embarrassing about al-Qa'ida operations, such as al-Qa'ida fund-raising in that country, what's the likelihood the security service conducting the questioning would freely pass that information back to the Agency?

One senior manager from the post-9/11 era in CTC remem-bers the frustrations of waiting for detailed debriefing informa-tion from foreign services. "I remember waiting weeks for that first debriefing report [from a detainee sent to a friendly Middle Eastern country in late 2001]. The reports we got were full of holes. 'This is bullshit. We have to do it ourselves.'"

The prosecution option raised another potential complication. Debates about whether to try al-Qa'ida suspects—particularly those detained at Guantanamo Bay, which opened for al-Qa'ida detainees in 2002—cropped up, but domestic politics intervened: some US officials cited security at potential al-Qa'ida trials as a roadblock to prosecutions. Few if any CIA officials, though, raised this concern as key when they thought about the prospect of sending these al-Qa'ida detainees to the US for prosecution. In the firestorm that followed 9/11, the primary question most had was instead how to extract intelligence from prisoners who would immediately, when they entered the US justice system, acquire a lawyer and decline to speak.

There was the question, too, about whether the United States could build cases against some of these prisoners, like the pre-9/11 questions about whether Washington had an ironclad case against bin Ladin. The CIA had built intelligence investigations around the detainees, information that was secretly acquired about the prisoners and their knowledge of al-Qa'ida. Prosecution assumed that the Department of Justice and FBI had open investigations on these detainees and what the Bureau would call "paper," an indictment that would give the government the formal legal authority to charge detainees. In many cases, there was no paper.

This legal question was critical. Intelligence is often fragmentary, leading an analyst to estimate the rough outlines of what he knows and where the gaps lie. It's not even close to the exhaustive investigation of every contact, every phone number, every bank account, every move that a prosecutor might seek, because intelligence collectors are operating at a distance in countries where they can't acquire even close to what an FBI investigator can amass in an investigation on US soil. Without the first-hand capability to search and seize information from a prisoner in friendly territory, with the support of US courts and state and local law enforcement agencies—not to mention the volumes of publicly available information on the Internet—investigators in America face more legal restrictions than the CIA overseas but also far more access to the individuals they are pursuing. Fragmentary intelligence, then, offers shadows of plots, slices of terror organizations. By contrast, evidence collected for a courtroom is supposed to go into far more detail: evidence that proves beyond a reasonable doubt. In many cases, the Agency and the US government had intelligence that was easily sufficient to judge with confidence that a particular detainee had al-Qa'ida ties. But even high-quality intelligence files often didn't reach the standard for courtroom evidence.

Congress and others in Washington, and around the country,

were adamant that the United States had long treated al-Qa'ida as a law enforcement problem before the 9/11 attacks. For the few terrorists we want to prosecute, the thinking went, we will prosecute in the United States. For those captured overseas, America should send them someplace else, for prosecutions in their home countries. Anything that had the then-unacceptable scent of those pre-attack days, when capture operations were viewed through this legal lens, was seen as too conservative, too narrow. Try to build cases for the Department of Justice? Few people wanted that.

They moved Abu Zubaydah to Catseye in April 2002. His transfer was scripted; it was one rare area in the rendition, detention, and interrogation of prisoners in which the Agency had years of experience. The CIA already had standard procedures, from the pre-9/11 years, for transporting prisoners from capture locations back to their home countries. Some of these transfers happened quickly: host governments that participated in capture operations didn't want to sit on al-Qa'ida detainees for more than a few days partly because they didn't want to answer questions, including from international human rights organizations, about what would happen to a detainee. It was better, from their perspective, to have the prisoner quickly whisked away to a silent location, with no publicity. If anybody asked questions, the answer could be simple: he's not here. The CIA often paid for the cooperation that led to these takedowns, money that was a significant motivator for cash-strapped security services.

Captures typically didn't happen without planning, and renditions didn't happen overnight, so dedicated rendition teams from the Agency had time to travel to the capture country to arrange aircraft transfers. The detainee would be strip-searched before the flight, then blindfolded and tethered within the aircraft. This policy of limiting risk on flights was also the motivation for diapering detainees; there were no bathroom visits on the flights. For food and liquids, detainees received only Ensure and water.

To counter inevitable questions later about the condition of detainees when they were transferred by CIA, and to ensure no mistreatment during travel (sometimes a day or more), the detainees were photographed naked before they got on the transport aircraft and after they arrived at the final destination. Another motivation for these before-and-after photographs had to do with the countries of origin. Some came from countries with questionable human rights records; some had been held and questioned by those countries' security services for periods ranging from a few days to a month. The CIA didn't want to take the chance that someone—including the detainees them-selves, whenever they would be shifted from CIA custody—would claim abuse. A medic described scars, tattoos, and other distinguishing features, and the photos covered all angles, back, front, left side, right side. When the flight landed, the process was reversed, with more photos to answer any future allega-tions of abuse.

Renditions also included body-cavity exams, to ensure they had not inserted either explosive devices or weapons into them-selves. One participant in the interrogations in those early years suggests that those probes might have been the source of detainee claims later that they had been sexually abused.*

---

* In a letter to the Department of Justice in September 2015, Amnesty International referred to rectal exams conducted with "excessive force." The letter asserts that senior CIA officials were advised of excessive rectal exams of two detainees "held at Detention Site Cobalt, believed to be in Afghanistan—information that appears not to have resulted in any sanction. One of the detainees, Mustafa al-Hawsawi was later diagnosed with "chronic hemorrhoids, an anal fissure, and symptomatic rectal prolapse."

In some instances, he says, the examining medics used rubber gloves without lubricants to humiliate the detainees. Perhaps this was their opportunity for what they might have seen as their tiny slice of vengeance.

Another rendition team would be prepared at the host airport after the flight, for the transfer to the black site. Again, the detainee would be strip-searched. Once the detainee arrived, he would be given a day or so to decompress. Then, the team began the assessment. How is this guy going to hold out? How nervous is he? Will he fold? And if he doesn't, how far do we have to go to get him to some level of compliance with our requests for information?

As Abu Zubaydah's health improved in the spring of 2002, even before his transfer, he was questioned. Those first sessions were jointly conducted, with both FBI and CIA officers present. This was well before the Agency considered a detention and interrogation Program; the assumption was that joint teams might combine the two agencies' complementary skills. Some judged that Abu Zubaydah might end up in US federal courts, and a US prison, as had happened with terrorists before 9/11. For any court case, FBI information from agents willing to be questioned on the stand would be crucial.

The pairing of the two agencies made sense for other reasons as well, at least on paper. The Bureau, because of its years of following al-Qa'ida before 9/11 and its experience building detailed legal cases against terrorists, had deep knowledge of the group; some agents and analysts had years of expertise. Further, the FBI is renowned for its interviewing techniques. Bureau agents train and practice building rapport with a wide variety of white-collar

criminals, drug dealers, foreign intelligence agents—and terrorists. That rapport-building approach often works, and coupled
with the Bureau's painstaking, methodical questioning, designed
to cover every angle and leave no gaps in court prosecutions,
Bureau agents rightly pride themselves on being some of the
government's most professional questioners.

Despite the glaring differences in interrogation philosophy
between the CIA and the FBI, that period of early FBI participation in Abu Zubaydah's debriefings wasn't without successes.
Before the Department of Justice ever formally authorized harsh
interrogation techniques, in the beginning Abu Zubaydah had
been subjected to sleep deprivation. Among the most effective
methods for breaking down a detainee's will, sleep deprivation
became a key component of the suite of interrogation techniques,
far more significant and common than waterboarding.

This wasn't just a matter of limiting a detainee's sleeping
hours. It was a calculated series of steps over days or more, to
the point where a detainee would lose track of time and gain an
insatiable need to rest. For one, the detainee might be forced to
stand for lengthy periods of time, hands shackled above so he
could not lie down. The duration of deprivations periods would
be determined by the joint interrogation teams, with physicians'
participation, but those periods might include staggered deprivation over days and sometimes extending to more than a week.

Further, the length of time between rest periods for the
detainee might be varied, contributing to a profound sense of
disorientation. For example, because the detainee had no access
to clocks, watches, or even natural light, he would not have a
good sense of how time was elapsing. He might be told that he
would sleep for an extended time and then be woken up two
hours later and assured that he had gotten a full night's rest. As

the need for sleep grew acute, his willingness to sacrifice bits of information—not full plots, but even seemingly minor details about an individual he'd met a year before—grew. Sleep deprivation became one of the top two or three methods among the ten techniques approved by the Department of Justice.

For Abu Zubaydah, as with other detainees, the interrogation team discussed how to handle him and what his resistance posture would be, according to one observer. In the midst of his disoriented state, Abu Zubaydah talked about what he described as "dreams of dirty bombs" (presumably a WMD) in the United States. Not much during that period could have elicited more interest: it came from the most senior al-Qa'ida member the Agency had in custody, coupled with a threat about a possible WMD follow-on to the 9/11 attacks. The interrogation team didn't want to let Abu Zubaydah off the hook for long; they had to pursue the threat, they thought.

They wove their strategy into follow-on conversations with Abu Zubaydah, telling him that these fragments of dreams were a message from Allah, who was telling him that it was acceptable for him to unburden himself of what he knew. Abu Zubaydah initially said he had in mind a recruit he sent to Khalid Shaykh Muhammed, but he said he was too tired to talk further. The interrogators contrived a plan to keep the conversation going. Rather than allow Abu Zubaydah a full night's sleep—delaying the interrogation and potentially giving him the chance to regain strength and the will to resist—they told him he could sleep. After just a few hours they woke him up, but they started the "new" day with the same routine that any day would begin with, leading him to believe he had been sleeping through the night.

At this point, after the artificially abbreviated rest, Abu Zubaydah provided one of the tiny fragments of information—not the full story, but a piece—that pointed the Agency to Jose

Padilla, an American citizen who was arrested shortly after, when he attempted to enter the United States via Chicago. It's not clear why Abu Zubaydah spoke. Did his priorities shift in the midst of exhaustion? Did he, like detainees who followed, feel that the small piece he gave up was inconsequential, a way to keep the interrogators at bay while he withheld other information he thought was more valuable? He was never transparent.

What he said wasn't nearly enough though, at least not for an impatient group of Agency officials reviewing his debriefings from afar. The Agency's leadership didn't see the partnership with the FBI as a good option, for a variety of reasons. The initial debriefings with the FBI were not going well, partly because the Agency did not believe the CIA interrogators had the time to develop rapport with Abu Zubaydah; the thought that the next plot might be in the offing, especially in those early days, always created a climate of urgency, of immediate action. Meanwhile, personality conflicts led to divisions between representatives of the two Agencies, and there were disagreements over who would manage the interrogations at the site. The Agency managers didn't believe Abu Zubaydah was developing a relationship with the key FBI interlocutor, as the FBI agents insisted.

The friction between the FBI and CIA should not have been surprising. The Bureau had extensive interviewing and interrogation experience; questioning suspects is one of the main elements of a successful special agent's career. The Agency had limited expertise. The joint-team approach never worked, from the perspective of Agency officers who were working at headquarters and field sites at that time. Bureau headquarters, steeped in operating on US soil under US law—and presenting evidence in US courts—was never comfortable with the Agency's evolving methods.

One individual involved in the Abu Zubaydah interrogations

thought part of the problem stemmed from the groups' differ-ent goals. "My thought is that the CIA was focused on the next attacks and the FBI was looking to build a case," he later said, echoing a divide that had plagued FBI-CIA relations for decades. In the Agency's eyes, intelligence about future targets, al-Qa'ida members—any tiny clue about the al-Qa'ida apparatus—was the prospect, not evidence.

Agency officials do not criticize FBI director Robert Muel-ler for the Bureau's refusal to participate in the program of harsh interrogations, including the EITs that followed through the lat-ter months of 2002. He is seen as one of the smartest, most com-mitted public servants of that era. He was also extremely close to CIA director Tenet. Agency senior officials saw Mueller as a seri-ous agent for change at the Bureau, not an impediment to CIA-FBI cooperation. Rather than a leadership divide, then, Agency officials see the CIA's development of the Program, despite the Bureau's refusal to participate, more as an indicator of the CIA's DNA during that era, and how it differed from the FBI's ethos. "If nobody else will do it, we will," Agency officials continued to believe, even as they initiated techniques the FBI would never use or participate in. Within the CIA there was a commitment to take the fight to Al-Qa'ida with that attitude.

Mueller no doubt foresaw what would happen down the road when the interrogation techniques inevitably became pub-lic knowledge, when the national temperature cooled and differ-ent players critiqued the Program.* "He saw it coming," said one

---

* One senior Program manager remembers that Mueller later spoke with a senior CIA official about rejoining the interrogations, though the Bureau always dis-tanced itself from the aggressive interrogation techniques. The Agency declined, and FBI officers never visited Program facilities again.

CIA officer who worked with him. Agency officials also saw the same Program downsides, and decided to proceed anyway. "The Agency kept everybody else away," says one field veteran from that era. "Fundamentally, that's where mistakes were made." Again and again, the single-minded drive to hunt al-Qa'ida— and the White House message to use every method authorized by the law—would push the Agency to legal boundaries.

Agency officials felt the ever-present pressure of time passing during the spring of 2002, after Abu Zubaydah's transfer to Catseye. The leviathan of US intelligence collection capabilities, from intercepts of emails and phone calls to the recruitment of new al-Qa'ida informants and partnerships with foreign security services, was starting to allow analysts to build a vast storehouse of information about al-Qa'ida. The Agency, though, still had a limited knowledge of the adversary they now pivoted to destroy, and especially about how al-Qa'ida was organized, who the key players were, and how they operated. As Abu Zubaydah recovered, and the Agency finally had its first senior al-Qa'ida leader to fill out gaps in the understanding of al-Qa'ida, his continued refusal to divulge what he knew, beyond the summer of 2002, frustrated Agency operators. What if there's an attack tomorrow and he knows some of the details, many wondered? What will we say then? Meanwhile, from the president on down, senior officials were asking the same question, frequently: What is Abu Zubaydah saying? When the White House would ask questions about Abu Zubaydah's revelations, remembers one former senior operations officer, "[The CIA] has nothing."

Abu Zubaydah's personal background soon captured the attention of some CIA executives, pushing the drive to interrogate him. There was reporting that he had traveled to St. Louis, for example, years earlier. In any investigation of al-Qa'ida plots

and plotters, one of the first questions intelligence professionals try to answer is whether the plots and plotters have tentacles
reaching directly into the United States. Phone contacts. Email
lists. Co-conspirators. In Abu Zubaydah's case, investigators
were driven to determine whether that travel to America had any
operational implications. They had to prove the negative, one
of the toughest tasks in the intelligence world. It wasn't just the
mission to know whether he had developed some operational
contacts in America; it was the mission to show, with confidence,
that he hadn't. In those post-9/11 days, no avenue that touched
the United States in any way would go unexplored. So interrogators pushed Abu Zubaydah about his days in America. Over
time, this turned out to be a dead end. It had been years before.
There was nothing useful to learn, but there was no way to know
without a relentless pursuit down every intelligence avenue.

And then there were the bigger, strategic, questions at the
heart of the post-9/11 pursuit of al-Qa'ida. Who is this new
terror adversary most Americans hadn't even heard of before
the attacks? How well do we know this group and its members? How do they think? How well have we penetrated them,
and where are the gaps in our knowledge? Said one seasoned
operator, describing the CIA's al-Qa'ida picture then, "We just
didn't have great [al-Qa'ida] sources. We were in the same boat
in August of 2002 as we had been a year earlier. The reason is
that our sources were too peripheral. We needed to penetrate the
inner circle."

Later, the CIA's penetration of al-Qa'ida with human sources
would improve, but that was still to come. "We had to do something different," this officer said. The "something different"
became the Program, developed in the midst of an Agency that
knew it could not depend on a stable of human informants to
give up the secrets of al-Qa'ida, and the next plot. With that in

mind, the CIA pushed to grow an entirely new stream of intelligence reporting: detainee intelligence.

Back at headquarters, the consensus among senior officers was quickly crystallizing through the spring and into the summer. We can't afford to be sitting with a detainee who may have information about another attack and allow that attack to happen without doing everything we can, some Agency leaders thought. The question was simple: How can we make him talk? One official with responsibility for creating the Program captured the emerging thinking about Abu Zubaydah in a single sentence: "We had to change the equation," he said more than a decade later, characterizing the thoughts around the deliberations surrounding that first interrogation in 2002. The Agency was headed into uncharted territory. "We thought about killing them [before]," recounts one CTC manager. "We hadn't thought about this."

Through that summer, CIA officials sought guidance from the Department of Justice about two broad questions. First, what did US law say about the treatment of prisoners, and how should US law apply to Abu Zubaydah and other detainees? And second, if the Agency received authorization to take aggressive steps with Abu Zubaydah, exactly which steps would be authorized under US law?

By August 2002, this question of what was legally authorized in CIA interrogations was clarified. In the August memorandum, DoJ formally certified a list of interrogation methods the Agency could use against al-Qa'ida prisoners. Before that memorandum, though, Abu Zubaydah had already faced pressure from interrogators, including sleep deprivation; and he had offered some information. Using the information he provided before the formal DoJ approval, then, turned out to be a misleading litmus test for whether he would provide answers when he wasn't under duress, and when he wasn't subject to the formal Program techniques. He did provide answers before, but those answers were mixed in with coercion.*

Some of those who would become CIA interrogators thought the rapport-building approach they had witnessed with Abu Zubaydah wouldn't produce results. From their perspective, he didn't care; he wasn't getting out from US custody, and he didn't have incentives to be truthful. His priority, they thought, motivated him: he wanted to protect al-Qa'ida, and his peers in the group. Not long after his capture, they decided he was shutting down. He turned to his interrogators and validated their view that he was through with answering questions. "You might as well go home and have babies," he said. They were wasting their time, they thought.

The interrogators believed Abu Zubaydah was toying with them. Sometimes he would offer simple yes-or-no answers. Sometimes he would spin lengthy tales about a terrorist he knew, only to close the story later, after what the interrogators believed was a long-winded effort to waste time. "That guy I was talking to you about," he'd say, "he died in 1998." The stories sometimes led nowhere. Further, they thought he was stringing them along by suggesting that if they spent more time with him, building rapport, he would eventually give up the mother lode, that some of them had a special relationship with him. The CIA

---

* There is widespread confusion—and disagreement—about the information Abu Zubaydah offered before and after he was subjected to tough interrogation techniques; some of that confusion stems from the fact that the legal guidance from DoJ didn't arrive until August 2002 and CTC didn't formally establish a unit for interrogations until December 2002. By that time, Abu Zubaydah had already undergone interrogation measures—including sleep deprivation—but the formal Program, as it later came to be known, had not started. Saying, then, that he offered valuable information before the institution of the Program is accurate; saying that the information he offered came entirely without duress is not.

interrogators came to believe it was all a ruse, that he was leading them down paths that went nowhere, all in an effort to keep
them at bay.

A criminal's intent in cooperating might be to avoid jail time.
For al-Qa'ida detainees, many wanted to protect colleagues,
or guard information about attack planning. The interrogators
wanted to shift these priorities: sleep deprivation might lead a
detainee to try to figure out how to balance his interest in protecting colleagues with his increasing drive for rest. As a first
step, some detainees would try to offer up details that they did not
believe would compromise their primary interests. Abu Zubaydah, for example, offered tidbits that were technically accurate
but worthless, and he spoke in short sentences, presumably to
avoid revealing too much or falling into traps. He might identify
an individual in a photo but add that he knew no detail. Or he
would open up about dead former colleagues, knowing nothing
he could say would result in their capture.

There wasn't the possibility of a deal with the detainees, and
Program interrogators didn't offer deals. In a rare exception
(possibly the only exception), one former Program administra-
tor remembers the Agency sending a fluent Arabic speaker and
longtime CIA operations specialist to talk with Khalid Shaykh
Mohammed. The offer to KSM: if you give us the information
we're looking for, we will arrange for you to send a letter to your
family, and you can receive photos in return. The administra-
tor remembers KSM's response, a snapshot of why the al-Qa'ida
detainees were so difficult to work with: "No," KSM answered,
"Allah will take care of my family. I don't have to worry."

Abu Zubaydah didn't get any deals. Nonetheless, he developed a relationship with interrogators, even as he evaded them.
During those frustrating sessions, Abu Zubaydah sometimes
charmed them. One recalls his interactions with this new phe-

nomenon, a core al-Qa'ida member. "He reminded me of what you would expect a Jedi knight to be like if you had him in your basement. Incredible charisma. Poise." But occasionally, he would drop the pretense and slouch back in a chair, one hand over his crotch. "He was charming 99 percent of the time," said one interrogator, "until he was thuggish." He also had a sense of humor, even crude humor. At one point, the questioning turned to one of the Agency's priority areas, the concern that al-Qa'ida had acquired nuclear materials. Abu Zubaydah leaned forward, as if he was preparing to confide in them. Instead, he released a loud fart. "Now that's nuclear," he laughed.

Abu Zubaydah's modest command of English facilitated his interaction with interrogators, starting with his first days through the tough tactics that followed later, and his English language skills improved with time. Some conversations were in Arabic, but eventually the interrogators insisted on English: there were many observers at the black sites, including those outside the room, and the management team overseeing the interrogations wanted to ensure that the non-Arabic speakers could follow what was going on, in real time.

In one of the thousands of tragedies and ironies that would mark the years-long counterterror campaign, one of those observers would later die in a suicide bombing conducted by an al-Qa'ida member who had lured the Agency into believing he was clean.

The suicide attacker was an al-Qa'ida plant, a double agent pretending to cooperate with the Agency while he prepared all along to sacrifice his life at a compound not far from the border of Pakistan. Among the nine dead that day was Jennifer Matthews, a forty-five-year-old mother of three who had been one of the experts on al-Qa'ida before 9/11 and key in the hunt for al-Qa'ida members. She ran that CIA base, collecting intelligence through methods including debriefing sources. The Jordanian al-Qa'ida recruit responsible for her death and others was believed to be a key informant, and he passed through the base checkpoints quickly, detonating his suicide bomb inside the compound.

Meanwhile, tantalizing clues swirled around Abu Zubaydah. Months after his imprisonment, and following rough interrogation techniques that had begun supplying more information, the gaps in the CIA's knowledge about al-Qa'ida drove the same relentless urgency. CTC personnel at headquarters uncovered short videos Abu Zubaydah had made, celebrating what appeared to be future terror attacks. Headquarters officials, convinced Abu Zubaydah had withheld information about future plots even as field interrogators found him to be more open, pressed for a return to the use of interrogation techniques. The field officers resisted. They sometimes judged that headquarters analysts were too arrogant in assessing what detainees knew. In one case, a Program manager remembers an analyst judging that it was "inconceivable" that Abu Zubaydah would know nothing about a subject. The field's response: we can't proceed based on guesses; we need information to box in the detainee; without that information, we don't have a credible way to determine whether he's lying. The field won that round.

As it turns out, Abu Zubaydah had his own explanation for the stored videos. Like many terror leaders, he was focused not just on planning and executing attacks but on recruiting followers and proving their bona fides to wealthy donors—typically from the Arabian Gulf area, in the case of al-Qa'ida—who want proof that their donations to the cause won't go to waste. For these donors, the al-Qa'ida message that Western troops and culture should be expelled can be compelling. Western troops and culture should be expelled from the lands of Islam because the West is, in their view, shifting these lands toward a worldview

that favors culture that degrades women and families and cor-
rupt governments that have allowed Western intervention. Al-
Qa'ida represented to donors one entity that has stood up to the
West with the 9/11 attacks and a promise to adhere only to the
tenets of Islam, not to any Western political philosophy, creed, or
cultural pollution.

These donors, though, wanted proof that the terror group
they were helping to fund would act. As it turned out, Abu
Zubaydah didn't have any specific attacks he was commemo-
rating in those tapes. Instead, it was a classic case of terrorist
chest-thumping, to persuade the organization that they are on
the side of victory and that despite setbacks God has ordained
them to win.

8

The Definition of Pain

The early meetings about the Program were not widely advertised in CIA senior circles, nor were they broadly attended. The full Counterterrorism Center leadership team, along with executives from across the Agency (public affairs, general counsel, staff assistants, military and FBI representatives, etc.) gathered every evening for the so-called "5 o'clock" meeting, also referred to as the "Small Group" despite participation that might number two or three dozen, including backbenchers standing along the wall in the director's seventh-floor conference room. This group was not representative of the much smaller core of counterterrorism professionals who formed the circle that Tenet turned to on high-profile counterterrorism questions. Everybody had a Top Secret clearance, but even with that, there were still higher classifications of secrecy, from Special Access Programs to "compartmented" programs to "cabinets" of information from highly sensitive human sources. "You're not cleared for that" was common for CIA officers, despite their Top Secret clearances.

From the earliest days of the internal deliberations, lawyers were central, partly because of the CIA's never-ending drive for more documentation. The senior-most attorneys in the Office of General Counsel, Scott Muller and John Rizzo, were core players in 2002, when the Agency was in close consultation with the Department of Justice about the first legal guidance for this wholly new interrogation program, a US government initiative so unheard of that it required foundational legal reviews about whether it even complied with federal law and presidential authority. Even earlier, when the idea of using enhanced interrogation techniques was first broached on the Agency's seventh floor, Tenet had a senior attorney in the room, listening to the explanation of what the operators were proposing to do. An attendee at one of those early meetings remembers the director leaning over to his legal adviser with a question that would crop up frequently in the coming years. "Make sure this is legal," he remembers Tenet saying. Everybody knew the Agency was headed for a new era.

The level of compartmentation for the Program—in other words, the extent to which it was segregated from discussion outside small, select groups at the Agency—was so high that even the executive assistants, or EAs, along the seventh-floor leadership corridor often did not have access to information about it. As gatekeepers and document reviewers for the Agency's senior executives, they typically reviewed a wide variety of sensitive information before deciding how, and whether, to send it to the Agency's most senior officials. Even sensitive operational information about informants overseas went through the EA filters. Not the Program, though; it remained segregated. EAs might hear references to it in meetings or comments in hallways, but they were not privy to details, not just for security reasons but also to shield them from what CIA executives knew would eventually lead to sharp questioning of the Agency.

The five o'clock meetings covered highly sensitive issues, including the secretive hunt for individual al-Qa'ida members, how the Agency was acquiring global financial information, and what the director might say to a foreign leader or, often, to President Bush the following morning. But even those meetings, focused on a wide range of operational activities around the globe, didn't touch on the detainee Program. Instead, they convened afterward, when a few officials at the five o'clock would file into Director Tenet's office a few steps across the interior corridor from the conference room. "Let's go back to my office," he would say, and a handful of officials, or fewer, would walk across the inner corridor to his office just a few feet away. This was another indication that, even then, senior officials were well aware of the sensitivity of the Program. The Program wasn't a secret; everyone around the table knew that the CIA kept al-Qa'ida detainees. But it was sensitive, and highly so.

The tight circle, while it did not include every senior operations manager in the chain of command, did include those officials who had hunted al-Qa'ida before the attacks. And they would not stop before they gutted the al-Qa'ida organization. It is not clear that the Program would have gone in a different direction had a broader circle of advisers weighed in. It is, however, clear that the hardened counterterrorism operators who lost to al-Qa'ida on September 11 would not face many hurdles in getting the approvals they wanted to vastly expand the limits of the CIA's authorities to pursue al-Qa'ida afterward, and to piece together the Program. Some of these were the same decision-makers who had witnessed the hands-tied limitations of the pre-attack era. They were determined not to repeat the mistakes of caution and risk-avoidance.

The small group might seem unusual for its lack of reliance on the chain of command, but it reflected a few realities in the executive corridor of CIA's elite that were well known within the Agency and especially along its corridors of power. First, Tenet's leadership style was always personal, always engaged with whatever level of the Agency he thought was reliable and could answer his questions and requirements. He had served in small staffs, in Congress and in the White House; his background hadn't been in huge bureaucracies. His personality type, too, led him to build a small, trusted circle. He was larger than life, committed to the counterterrorism mission, personally interested in and involved with counterterrorism officials, and on a first-name basis with all of them. As the counterterrorism effort mushroomed, and as the Program evolved, he leaned on people he knew, especially those directly involved in the fight and those below the senior executives who occupied the power suites in the Agency's executive wing.

Tenet bypassed some leadership, and reached down further into the bureaucracy, partly because he trusted and depended on Cofer Black, who ran the Counterterrorism Center before and after 9/11, until mid-summer 2002. He had been the perfect partner to help Tenet raise the alarm about al-Qa'ida before the attacks, as Black gave Tenet the bare-knuckled global fight he wanted; it was Black who set the tone in the Counterterrorism Center for aggressive action, always, and who raised the Center's profile initially. With Black still at the helm, Tenet didn't need to assemble a huge command chain for decisions. Instead, he leaned directly on Black. The Counterterrorism Center willingly followed.

This direct line to CTC's leadership remained in place when Black left in 2002. His successor, Jose Rodriguez, made key decisions as the Program grew, and continued in Black's tradition with his powerful, aggressive counterterrorism approaches and attitudes that permeated the operational DNA of the Center at a level below the Agency's seventh-floor executive suites. Short and stocky, with jet-black hair and a mustache to match, Rodriguez reveled in the operational decisions of a CTC world that was high risk, high return. He wasn't easy to anger, but he was quick to decide. Bring him a thorny operational problem from a field office—how to deal with a difficult foreign intelligence partner, for example—or a tough internal bureaucratic struggle, and you could be assured that he would move without too much red tape or endless consultations.

Though Rodriguez became a key architect of the Program when he stepped in, other senior seventh-floor executives who sat between Tenet and him were not. Rodriguez was always a decisive, damn-the-torpedoes leader, willing to take risks on covert actions despite the likelihood that his judgments would be reviewed, and sometimes harshly critiqued, by later generations. He wanted action. In a sign of the determination of that time, Rodriguez, fifteen years removed from those days, remains unapologetic. Others explain that at the time, no options were good.

Rodriguez never pretended to be more than what he was: an operator who didn't care about Washington niceties. Despite a law degree, he had a well-founded reputation as a quick decision-maker who didn't mind dirty choices and high stakes. "Fuck it," he might say in the midst of a tough decision, "what else are we gonna do?" And then he'd move on. He had a sense of humor, even in difficult moments, that was unrivaled among his CIA peers. He hated insider Washington representational duties, so he'd come up with excuses to avoid them. "I'm from Puerto Rico," he'd say, "and I don't talk pretty. You go talk to the White House." Or, referring to the fact that he was prohibited from acknowledging publicly his CIA affiliation, "I'm undercover. I've operated overseas all my life. I can't go brief the Congress." Complete nonsense, as all his staff knew. But he was always funny, always ready to relieve the stress at the heart of the CIA's counterterrorism business.

Rodriguez and his subordinates were under pressure to deliver results because of the already high profile of Abu Zubaydah and the passage of time. It wasn't that Rodriguez favored instituting the interrogation plan as a result of the pressure. It was more that he, and others in Washington including White House officials, saw Abu Zubaydah as a potential key that would help the Agency accelerate its takedown of the al-Qa'ida network. Agency officials from that time acknowledge that their picture of al-Qa'ida, less than a year after the attacks, remained blurry. Intelligence officers use a standard phrase—"intelligence gaps"—to describe what they do not know. They saw Abu Zubaydah as a goldmine to close gaps.

Just as the Agency had no experience in building and maintaining an interrogation program, its lawyers faced a difficult decision in 2002. How do we, they would ask themselves, provide legal counsel on an issue so unusual and potentially explosive?

There were no illusions, despite the fact that America was less than a year out from 9/11, about the legal implications of subjecting detainees to harsh interrogations and solitary confinement outside a judicial process. Said one senior attorney, "I thought this sounded crazy when I first heard of it. Some of it sounded scary. And it wasn't something we were prepared to deal with.

I had to walk around the building [the CIA campus] to think about it." These questions became urgent after Abu Zubaydah's capture. The lawyers' decisions: How do we counsel the director? How do we involve the Department of Justice, and the DoJ legal arm, the Office of Legal Counsel, that sets US legal policy? They were in uncharted territory. As it turns out, that territory grew more convoluted, not less, as the years passed. From the start, this attorney remembers thinking, the Program "had trouble written all over it."

Lawyers read those lengthy technical legal treatises during those months, and they discussed their significance in the executive suites at the Agency's Langley campus. Counterterrorism professionals might not have read the Justice Department's dry analyses, but the language from a few critical passages did spread into everyday conversations in the wake of those first Justice opinions in August 2002. Those opinions are now declassified, and hotly debated among lawyers and human rights activists, but at the time they were the cornerstone of how the CIA understood Department of Justice guidance. Key phrases became part of how counterterrorism professions looked at the frame within which they had to develop the Program.

"We conclude below," the memorandum's drafters wrote, in the opening paragraph, "that Section 2340A [of the Convention against Torture, which is reflected in US law] proscribes acts inflicting, and that are specifically intended to inflict, severe pain or suffering, whether mental or physical." This emphasis on intent was critical. If the interrogators intended to elicit information without inflicting pain, but instead focused on harsh techniques that were designed to reduce the detainee to a feeling of helplessness or despair that would lead him to answer questions, the Agency Program complied with the law.

The legal memorandum later clarified the authors' interpretation of pain: "Physical pain amounting to torture must be equivalent in intensity to the pain accompanying serious physical injury, such as organ failure, impairment of bodily function, or even death." The document's drafters also clarified their interpretation of prolonged psychological harm. "Put another way, the acts giving rise to the harm must cause some lasting, though not necessarily permanent, damage. For example, the mental strain experienced by an individual during a lengthy and intense interrogation—such as one that state or local police might conduct upon a criminal suspect—would not violate Section 2340(2)."

This was another critical point: it wasn't just whether the interrogation techniques were unpleasant. It was about what the interrogators intended to do, and whether what they did caused short-term misery or long-term physical or mental problems. It provided the legal justification they needed to continue, without wiggle room that they believed would cause them trouble down the road, during the inevitable second-guessing about this new covert action. And intent is critical: if the interrogators intend only to reduce the detainee to a state of helplessness without causing lasting damage, the techniques were defensible in the eyes of the Program's architects. These simple judgments became widely known and discussed among nonlegal professionals who oversaw and ran the Program. Rarely had key phrases from legal documents become such common reference points in conversations across the Agency.

Behind those documents, however, was the broader, foundational presidential authorization, dating from the days after the attacks. Under the headline, "CIA Told to Do 'Whatever Necessary' to Kill Bin Laden," *Washington Post* staff writer Bob Woodward reported in October 2001 that President Bush had signed an order, known as a Presidential Finding, that directed the CIA to undertake "its most sweeping and lethal covert action since the founding of the agency in 1947, explicitly calling for the destruction of Osama bin Laden and his worldwide al Qaeda network, according to senior government officials." The article went on to detail the remarkable breadth of the order, which included authorization for the Agency to "attack bin Laden's communications, security apparatus and infrastructure." Some in the Agency later referred to this as "the gloves come off" memorandum.

Time and again, CIA officers through the management ranks point to presidential guidance as one of the pillars that later led them down the path to the Program. Said one senior interrogator, "We were asked by the president to do whatever it took within the law to save American lives." Most of these officers never met the president, but they took his words as a reflection of what America's highest-level officials wanted. "I just followed the president's lead," said another. They thought he reflected the tenor of the times, and the wishes of the American people.

The order not only served as the touchstone for the fine-tuned legal judgments that followed, it also gave Agency officers the sense that their aggressive actions in the coming years were supported by elected officials at the highest levels. The president ordered; they executed. Woodward reported one senior official saying, once again, "The gloves are off. The president has given the agency the green light to do whatever is necessary. Lethal operations that were unthinkable pre-September 11 are now underway." Before the attacks, that line was unbreachable. With the Bush order and the initial DoJ guidance, the tenor of the times remained what it had been immediately after 9/11. Do what you need to, within US law. And what you are proposing, in this instance, is within US law. Said one CIA officer, "At that time [of the memos], we could have done whatever we wanted, however we wanted. But we chose that route, through OLC [the Office of Legal Counsel, the policy element at the Department of Justice responsible for rendering formal legal opinions on the Program]." From the CIA's perspective, they were far from rogue; they were mainstream. By August 2002, the CIA was formally in the interrogation business.

CIA officers had no illusions that the Program would remain secret forever, and they didn't expect the authorizations to be viewed by critics as a blank check. One manager of the interrogation program had a placard in his office at that time: "There are no secrets," it said, a reminder that whatever the Agency did then, veiled from public view, would eventually be open to public judgment, and criticism. CIA covert actions—those secret activities its officers conduct overseas, at the direction of the president—almost never are, and the consequences of exposure of CIA's most controversial operations has long haunted the Agency and its partners. The discussions about black sites with foreign security services, then, included clear warnings about the risk of exposure. Some countries were involved in building their country's image, and its international reach, and they understood the implications of linkage with a program of secret CIA prisons. Nonetheless, they signed up, in another indication of how unified America and its allies were in the first couple of years after the attacks.

These profound legal judgments translated into critical participation in the Program's initial design—and its later evolution—by CTC's cadre of lawyers, who provided not only broad oversight for policy but also tactical reviews of policy implementation and even outgoing communications with the field. CTC lawyers were subordinate to the General Counsel's office but, in a unique arrangement, they sat in CTC offices, becoming part of the operational components at a tactical level so they could communicate with, and be part of the pulse of, everyday operations. The senior OGC "detailee" in the Center, in the coming years, would become one of the most critical players in the day-to-day translation of Justice's legal paperwork into real-world guidance to CIA interrogators.

These lawyers, on "detail" from the General Counsel's office to CTC, not only played twin roles in the Center on detention and interrogation operations but also a broader range of tough operational issues. Many had experience in some of the most critical decisions of the counterterrorism war. Their ability to influence what the CIA did—experience that was unparalleled—and their co-location inside CTC meant that they gained the trust of the Center's managers, who viewed them not as barriers to action or as a bureaucratic bottleneck but as invaluable partners who participated in countless discussions about Program implementation as CTC staff translated the memos into interrogation policy and practice.

Agency leaders quickly got over any reservations about proceeding with this new, controversial covert action. They saw a simple rationale for why the harsh interrogation tactics they would soon approve seemed defensible, even entirely appropriate given the mood of the country. "If we use tactics at the CIA that the US military uses to train its own personnel, we should be on solid ground," Agency leaders and counterterrorism managers thought. Early on, then, senior executives' conversations about how to design a more aggressive interrogation regime for Abu Zubaydah included references to the SERE program, the military Survival, Evasion, Resistance, Escape training that included subjecting trainees to harsh tactics, including waterboarding. SERE was designed to train personnel on how to evade and survive capture, and included resistance techniques for interrogation. As part of the training, SERE students undergo versions of the techniques themselves.

Among the CIA officers considering how to handle Abu

Zubaydah's intransigence, reverse-engineering SERE tactics seemed like a simple, straightforward option that could work and also shield the Agency from future criticism. Not only were there interrogators who were familiar with the tactics, but the ethical considerations didn't seem like insurmountable hurdles. In 2002, subjecting al-Qa'ida detainees to the same interrogation methods employed against US military trainees didn't raise significant concerns. Those officers contemplating using the SERE tactics did not at the time, though, have any sense of how quickly the national unity they felt behind the relentless al-Qa'ida hunt would begin to fray.

This thinking extended to CIA personnel who had themselves gone through SERE training. Like many other Agency staff who judged what they would say when the inevitable critiques of the Program began, one senior Agency executive who had served as special forces officer remembered his experiences with SERE training as a key factor in how he judged this unique CIA operation. Even for them, though, the step toward using these techniques outside US military training was a risky proposition. Said one senior CIA official who had undergone SERE techniques, "I think there was good, solid, actionable information that came out of there [the Program]. I thought, yeah, this is really uncomfortable, but you don't die. And it's one of those things every special ops guy and every aviator goes through. My view [of the interrogations] was that I was slightly positive."

The fact that SERE had been used for so long in the US military allowed Agency officers a simple answer to their own personal considerations about the ethics of the newly emerging Program. Its initiation, with the reverse-engineered SERE techniques at its core, never did include a structured, or in-depth, ethical debate among the Program's architects, either at the outset or as the Program developed. Tenet, during the initial stages, did not convene a formal planning-and-review team to create a lengthy planning document, or to review whether the Agency should even go down this path. Instead, the drive to maximize any advantage over the 9/11 killers, and the fact that the SERE techniques were viewed as acceptable probably helped ease any concerns. Officers then and now reflect on the ethical questions about their decisions, but those are personal reflections. Then, the emphasis was on action.

Lacking experience in the techniques, the Agency turned to advice from people they already knew who had experience with SERE school in the US military. Former CTC managers today say they found the guidance for developing the foundations of the Program in two psychologists who had deep experience in SERE techniques and who became the core of the Program's philosophy. Those two psychologists came to personify the distinctions between the unplanned detention and unstructured interrogation of that first prisoner and the evolution of the Program into a well-defined, headquarters-managed web of secret detention facilities and orchestrated interrogation practices. One CTC manager remembers the transition, echoing a sentiment many operators say they felt at the time. "It was when [the psychologists] got involved that I could sense people felt, at least we have people who've been in the SERE business. Setting left and right parameters, when you waterboard, when you don't. The Program was growing by leaps and bounds. There was an idea that they [Agency managers] wanted to standardize it."

To be clear, however, this wasn't a completely uncharted path for the Agency because of its preexisting contract relationship with one of the psychologists. He was simply reassigned from within the Agency to CTC's Special Missions Department to help with the Program. To add expertise, and to deal with the workload, he recommended another psychologist who was familiar with the SERE methodology. Together, they defined the underpinnings of the theory behind the Agency's emerging interrogation methodology, along with the combinations of techniques used in individual detainee cases, based on the prisoner's personality and level of resistance over time. Today, former senior officials routinely point to these two contractors as key to putting the program on a sounder, longer-term footing. Core to this maturation were a few characteristics that defined how officers viewed the Program's tactics and goals.

The SERE specialists, especially the first expert at Langley, were uniquely positioned, at a time when frustrations with Abu Zubaydah were running high. CIA officers judged that at least some of the detainees they would face had received training in counterinterrogation techniques. Part of their supposition was based on the seizure by British authorities in 2000 of what was called the "Manchester Manual," which was later found translated in other raids around the world. This handbook, widely cited afterward as a primer for al-Qa'ida members, included writings on interrogation mindsets and how a prisoner should conduct himself during detention. The intent of some of the instruction relates to guiding prisoners on how to limit disclosures that would damage terror operations. The manual also includes guidance on obtaining information that would help later persuade a court that the prisoner was subjected to abuse. In the opening of Lesson 18 of the manual, a chapter dedicated to prisons and detention centers, the trainee is advised:

- At the beginning of the trial, once more the brothers [the term al-Qa'ida members often used to refer to one another] must insist on proving that torture was

inflicted on them by State Security [investigators] before
the judge.

• Complain [to the court] of mistreatment while in prison.

The highly detailed manual also offers instruction to trainees on
what to expect during interrogation, and how to resist.

• In the beginning, the brother may not be treated harshly,
but rather kindly. He may be offered a chair with a cup
of tea or a drink. Then he would be asked to recall information that is useful to the interrogators. If the brother
refuses to offer any information and denies that he knows
anything, he is then treated harshly. He and his family may be cursed, he may be forced into submission by
following orders such as: face the wall, don't talk, don't
raise your voice. All of that is to frighten the brother.
The brother should refuse to supply any information and
deny his knowledge of the subject in question. Further,
the brother should disobey the interrogator's orders as
much as he can by raising his voice, cursing the interrogator back, and refusing to face the wall. The interrogator
would resort to beating the brother in order to force him
to obey. Thus, that attempt would fail.

• Within about a day, another session would be held with
the brother. Usually, in this session the brother would
be blindfolded, beaten, and tortured. He would be made
to believe that his role in the incidents has been learned
and that it is better if he talks. The cursing and torturing
would intensify, depending on what the brother reveals.
The brother should not disclose any information, no matter how insignificant he might think it is, in order not to
open a door that cannot be closed until he incriminates

himself or exposes his Organization. The interrogator
cannot obtain what he wants and extract any information
unless the brother talks. The brother may think that by
giving a little information he can avoid harm and torture.

The Agency had been concerned about how al-Qa'ida would
respond to interrogations for months, but those conversations
didn't lead to the planning the Agency had to do after the Abu
Zubaydah capture. In late 2001, well before Abu Zubaydah was
detained, the CIA "had tasked an independent contractor psychologist . . . to research and write a paper on Al-Qa'ida's resistance to interrogation techniques," according to an Inspector
General report. The title of that paper was telling: "Recogniz-
ing and Developing Countermeasures to Al-Qa'ida Resistance
to Interrogation Techniques: A Resistance Training Perspective."
Even earlier that year, CIA officials discussed their capture and
detention authorities (a formal term—the written authorization
received to conduct detention and interrogation operations), and
they spoke broadly about what standards they would strive to
meet. They knew they couldn't match the US Bureau of Prisons;
they initially spoke of meeting "U.S. POW Standards."

Now, less than six months after Abu Zubaydah's capture,
DoJ lawyers were about to provide their first answers to the
questions of how to interpret US law on interrogations and what
techniques were acceptable in the event detainees resisted interrogation. Agency officials thought Abu Zubaydah, and other
al-Qa'ida members, might have received training based on the
manual, but they weren't certain. At the very least, they believed
Abu Zubaydah was shutting down, and they were looking for a
way to change the dynamic with him. The initial mission of the
psychologist wasn't to interrogate him, but to review the man-
uals and determine if and how the Manchester Manual might

offer clues about his resistance, and to offer insights into what resistance behaviors the Agency could counter. Was he using the Manchester Manual's resistance strategies? For a psychologist trained in how thousands of US trainees had responded to SERE techniques, the next step was inevitable. If CIA prisoners were exhibiting resistance, perhaps based on training, what did the long history of the SERE school experience offer in terms of options to break that resistance? Again and again, one phrase cropped up: "We have to change the equation," said one of the Program sponsors. The CIA just didn't think they could wait.

The personal deliberation about whether to accede to the CIA's request to support the Program managers came to a close quickly. "Originally I said no," remembers one interrogator, when he was asked to transition to hands-on interrogations with Abu Zubaydah, as opposed to a hands-off advisory role. The senior Agency manager persisted with the request. " 'It's you or nobody,' " he was told. "I knew my life would be over," he says he thought when he got the request. "Then somebody leaned over and said if you're not willing to do it, how can we ask somebody else?" The interrogator, though, couldn't develop an entire new operation on his own, and he knew it then. Immediately, he asked for help, for a colleague with more experience. The expert he requested wasn't at the Agency then, but he arrived within a week, another indication of how quickly events moved during those times. The first conversations about using specific contractors to administer SERE techniques occurred in the early summer of 2002.

Before the DoJ memo in August, the two psychologists worked under CTC staff and lawyers and with CIA staff to come up with specific procedures for how to implement the list of interrogation techniques that fell under the DoJ legal finding. The list didn't include every step the CIA took that would differentiate Program prisons from a standard detention facility. For example, some aspects of the interrogation program were referred to as what were called "conditioning"—white noise to keep prisoners from communicating with each other and constant lighting to ensure that prisoners didn't know whether it was day or night. For the formal, physically harsh techniques that were approved by DoJ, the total number was eventually narrowed to the group that CIA officers came to refer to as Enhanced Interrogation Techniques, or EITs. Constant music wasn't on the list; sleep deprivation was.

The use of the word "enhanced" wasn't incidental. The Agency also used what they referred to as "standard" techniques that, in their view, did not "incorporate significant physical or psychological pressure," as interrogation guidelines described them. Those "standard" techniques included: isolation; sleep deprivation not to exceed seventy-two hours; deprivation of reading material; white noise at a decibel level calculated not to cause damage to the detainee's hearing; reduced caloric intake; and diapers for limited periods.

The harsher SERE-derived techniques formed the core of the CIA's request for DoJ guidance. If the Agency was going to base its new interrogation operations on specific techniques, the old hands who had gone through the searing after-action criticisms of earlier covert actions, particularly in Latin America, wanted written approval from DoJ lawyers. The SERE-derived techniques, then, were the formal basis of a written CIA memo to DoJ for a legal opinion. In essence, the CIA outlined what it wanted, including specific techniques, with DoJ then reviewing the request to determine whether each technique complied with the law. Without the DoJ opinion in writing there would not have been a formal interrogation process. But with DoJ approval, the Agency felt not only that the Program was on solid legal ground—according to the Constitution, federal statutes, and international obligations—but also solid moral footing.

The now highly controversial documents that underpinned the Program were dated August 1, 2002, and the formal Program started shortly after. The documents included a few basic components. First, there was the lengthy legal argument about why the Program complied with US law. For the interrogators themselves, the second major element of the DoJ documentation was more immediately critical: the listing of the ten techniques that were authorized by Justice. The techniques the Department of Justice approved as complying with US law in that fateful August memo included the following:*

- Attention grasp. Grabbing a detainee forcibly by the collar, pulling him closer to the interrogator to gain his attention.
- Cramped confinement. Placing a detainee in a dark, tight space.
- Insects (placing a detainee in a confinement box with insects).
- Facial hold. Holding a detainee's face immobile during questioning.
- Facial slap ("insult slap"). Slapping a detainee with spread fingers, to induce "shock, surprise, or humiliation," according to a DoJ memorandum.

---

* Later reports suggested that rectal rehydration—inserting fluids into a detainee via a rectal tube—was an interrogation tactic. CIA officers maintain that this was a medical procedure. Those CIA managers who commented on this controversy, up and down the CIA chain of command, were not aware of this procedure before they heard about it in media reports. Their view, generally, is that had they known of it when they were in the CIA management chain, they would have deferred to physicians about whether it was an appropriate treatment regimen for a prisoner.

- Sleep deprivation. Forcing detainees to remain upright and ensuring that they either did not sleep or slept for short periods, sometimes for days at a time.
- Stress positions. Uncomfortable positions in which a prisoner might be handcuffed, with his feet shackled to the floor, resulting in leg muscle fatigue.
- Wall standing. The detainee faces a wall, standing far enough out so that he has to reach to place his fingers against the wall in front of him.
- "Walling." Pushing a detainee against a flexible wall.
- Waterboarding.

Despite its later notoriety, waterboarding was not the most debated tactic at that time. During the approval process for the Program, and during subsequent exchanges with officials at the Department of Justice and the Bush White House, the tactic that led senior Administration officials to pause was more personal: nudity for prisoners. "It was the image, not the science," said one senior official, recollecting White House rejection of nudity as an interrogation measure. Most attribute the opposition as an indication not that the tactic was particularly more objectionable than others but that those who objected were making decisions based on sentiment.

Not all the techniques that were discussed in Washington became reality, partly because the interrogators didn't want them or feel they needed them. Earlier, at the outset of the program, the Agency had declined to use a few authorized techniques. Prisoners talked to the Red Cross about being held in what were called "confinement boxes," designed to stress a prisoner by holding him in a box small enough that he couldn't stretch. One early technique under consideration, for example, was adding harmless snakes and insects to the boxes, particularly for prisoners who showed unusual fear of them. One of the administrators of the Program reflects that the reasons for rejecting the technique weren't all philosophical. "We didn't want to clean up the mess from the crushed bugs," he later said. It wasn't clear that the insect ban was Agency-driven; others remember using insects as an interrogation technique as one of the options the White House took off the final list, despite the DoJ authorization of the technique as legal.

The Agency also never employed mock burial as an interrogation technique, despite the fact that they thought it would meet with DoJ approval. All along in the Program, its designers adhered to the practice of ensuring that techniques weren't revealed so that prisoners didn't know what awaited them. In this case, the idea would have been to reinforce in the prisoner's mind this theme of helplessness. "There is a way out," the message always was. "But it has to be through us."

The legal basis for the Program was in place. The first formal CIA cable authorizing this suite of techniques was sent in August 2002 to that initial black site, where interrogators were ready for Abu Zubaydah. Not all the techniques were on the table; with his leg continuing to heal, for example, the interrogators wouldn't use the stress position technique because of the potential to aggravate his injury. The other methods, though, were in play, including the most aggressive measure the Agency ever used: waterboarding.

9

The Second Wave

CIA interrogators were all too aware that they had broad gaps to fill, as the Agency's knowledge of al-Qa'ida was eerily modest. Post-9/11 concerns about catastrophic attacks, possibly including a WMD strike, had not subsided after the first al-Qa'ida take-downs in 2002–3.

In the lead-up to the capture operation, Abu Zubaydah had been a regular feature in the president's daily intelligence digest, the President's Daily Brief or PDB, often referred to by CIA officers as "the book." On the morning of the capture, analysts drafted another article for the book. In contrast to the regular updates on what Abu Zubaydah was doing, and how the hunt for him was closing in, this intelligence had a different angle. What does his capture mean? How will it affect the al-Qa'ida organization? And what will he tell us about the mystery that still surrounds this shadowy adversary?

CTC analysts struggled with the answers the night before the article appeared, going back and forth in their conversations about the significance of his takedown. The fact was, they didn't have a good enough understanding of al-Qa'ida's dynamics to know how to answer these basic questions. In retrospect, their inability to summarize the significance of his removal from al-Qa'ida's ranks was a reflection of how little they knew about al-Qa'ida. Tenet was frustrated: the answers had to get better.

The analysts' questions about what Abu Zubaydah said after his capture only intensified during that summer of 2002. As weeks and months passed without any answers, a shadow seemed to hang over the agency. "We have no time," one of the uppermost Agency leaders recalls thinking. Some thought that administration officials were too aggressive in asking about the results of the initial interrogations, but that wasn't the motivation. It was the Agency leaders themselves who wanted answers, and they didn't feel they could wait.

Washington too was jumpy, going into the fall of 2002. From September and into October, right after the initial Department of Justice documents finally reached Langley, the District of Columbia and the suburbs of Virginia and Maryland witnessed a three-week series of anonymous sniper strikes that left ten dead, initially with no clear motivation, geographic focus, or perpetrator. The attacks had nothing to do with al-Qa'ida, but that realization came slowly. The CIA immediately questioned whether, thirteen months after 9/11, individual al-Qa'ida members had shifted to seemingly random attacks on everyday Americans, in retrospect what would have been a harbinger of the homegrown terrorism to come later in the decade. Even after two killers were arrested and it was evident that they had no connections with al-

Qa'ida, CIA officers wondered whether bin Ladin and al-Qa'ida planners had taken note. Would they learn from the chaos that enveloped the region around Washington? Seeing the paralysis in the national capital region orchestrated by just two armed men operating from one vehicle, would they decide that less spectacular attacks would be the new wave? And who could stop them if they did resort to snipers?

One officer recalls preparing his family for an evacuation from their home in the event of the next attack. He spoke to his wife about taking them to stay with relatives, and they discussed making sure the gas tank was always half full and ensuring that there was ready-packed food. "If it hits," he remembers saying, "just get in the car and head west." Like almost everyone at Langley, he expected another strike, or worse; "bigger, better, badder," said some, especially if al-Qa'ida had obtained weapons of mass destruction.

Underpinning the years of concerns, and the decisions about Abu Zubaydah, was the one overriding certainty—or what officials then considered a certainty—that al-Qa'ida was bent on staging what the counterterrorism community called the Second Wave. It could be a WMD operation, an attempt to down a building with explosives-laden vehicles, or another air assault. There was clear evidence that Al-Qa'ida had researched all three, and early investigations revealed recruitment—and deployment—of operatives to conduct Second Wave attacks, including in the United States. "We were blind to attack number one," says one of the CTC managers from that era. "What makes you think there aren't ten other cells out there like that?"

The glaring gaps in knowledge about the Second Wave related to people and plots, or what types of targets the group's terrorists might already have surveyed or selected. During the mid-

2000s through the first decade of the twenty-first century, those threats focus on railways, planes, and the group's recruitment of mostly young men in Europe and America. In the months and first years after 9/11, the deepest concerns some CIA leaders had were much darker: What if al-Qa'ida has a bomb? And what if they use it? This concern wasn't purely theoretical, nor was it farfetched. Based on exploitation of sites in Afghanistan and al-Qa'ida contacts with scientists, the CIA knew that al-Qa'ida had been experimenting before the 9/11 attacks with new, novel methods, such as poisons.

The now-forgotten weapons of mass destruction (WMD) reports of the time fed this sense of urgency about Abu Zubaydah. Lost in the passing years of no major attacks is the uncertainty that surrounded CIA's questions about al-Qa'ida's access to even low-level weapons of mass destruction. One top CIA official from that period says, "The single most important thing that drove decisions at the most senior level [in the US government] was the concern that a follow-on attack would be WMD. Domestically, we had the Black Hole of Calcutta [referring to knowledge of al-Qa'ida activities in the United States]. We just didn't know." CIA executives never were consumed by Hollywood-style plots of stolen Russian suitcase nukes or underground Mafia networks funneling material to al-Qa'ida. Far more immediate were the twin threats of how far al-Qa'ida's anthrax program had progressed—were there samples unaccounted for somewhere, destined for use in an attack?—and whether the group had even a rudimentary nuclear capability, perhaps via a relationship with individuals in Pakistan's nuclear establishment.

It wasn't just the potential al-Qa'ida capabilities in these areas that concerned Agency officers. It was the belief that the group also had the intent to use whatever they could build or acquire on the black market, especially with rampant rumors about what was available in the messy aftermath of the Soviet Union's decline. In the intelligence world, the characteristics of capability plus intent, along with opportunity, are the charateristics that define threat.

Calls for an independent commission had already started in 2002, and late that year, congressional legislation signed by President Bush created the National Commission on Terrorist Attacks Upon the United States (the 9/11 Commission). The attacks were viewed as an intelligence failure, a conclusion later upheld by the Commission when it issued its report. Thomas Kean, the panel's chairman, summarized the views of how intelligence performed before the attacks: "We were unprepared. We did not grasp the magnitude of a threat that had been gathering over a considerable period of time. As we detail in our report, this was a failure of policy, management, capability, and, above all, a failure of imagination." Nobody on September 10 would have believed an attack would result, the following day, in the fall of the towers. Who could presume, they thought, that anthrax wouldn't be next, particularly given al-Qa'ida's research into special weapons and its linkages with scientists who might provide the expertise they needed? During the early 2000s, the Agency had even developed a relationship with outside fiction writers to think about scenarios that less creative analysts in Washington might never consider.

Nevertheless, the WMD threat from al-Qa'ida wasn't universally accepted among CTC experts. The rank-and-file operators, analysts, and managers in CTC did not always treat the WMD department with great respect, but it was clear that Director Tenet held the WMD program and its officers in high regard.

And that he was driven by the threat. The officers themselves were viewed as outliers among more conventional analysts, and they were sometimes even ridiculed for chasing wisps of intelligence smoke while other officers hunted what they thought were more tangible al-Qa'ida plots and plotters. In the relatively small, and sometimes personalized and idiosyncratic environment of the Agency, this was one of many circumstances in which leadership personalities influenced events. And, as Agency senior officials saw it, the nascent WMD program in CTC had leadership and driving personalities in spades. The director's worries about WMD led him to believe the Agency needed to push detainees for information. The officers who worked for him had the ingenuity and drive to show why those worries were grounded in some reality.

Leading the WMD group was the intrepid, imaginative field officer Rolf Mowatt-Larssen, who was known widely as a Tenet favorite because he so doggedly pursued the elusive WMD threads as if each one was a guaranteed intelligence goldmine. Mowatt-Larssen didn't need much encouragement from Tenet. Clearly, to anyone who witnessed him in action, Mowatt-Larssen not only believed in the WMD mission but also had the drive and expertise to own the program he led. Aside from his knowledge and authority, he also had another critical personality attribute that helped him succeed: he didn't bristle much at the ridicule of his peers. Nor did he seem to revel in it. He never appeared either to care or particularly notice. Other CTC officers could snipe because they thought the WMD team hyped the threat; Mowatt-Larssen and his subordinate managers built a team that applied a different metric: if we're right in even one out of a hundred cases, this is all worth it.

The information Mowatt-Larssen and his team developed and provided to Tenet proved to be one of the most important factors that influenced the director on how to handle the detentions and interrogations. The anthrax worries were, if anything, more severe, and more pressing, than the nuclear concerns. Some of them centered on one individual, a biochemist trained in the United States who was in the midst of developing an anthrax program for al-Qa'ida that the CIA knew little about. The hunt for details about that program—not just about its history but about whether scientists had developed strains, or even whether there were extant samples in al-Qa'ida's possession—remained a priority. Those WMD concerns, particularly the investigation of an anthrax lab in Afghanistan, contributed to the overall sense that if the Agency didn't move quickly, the next attack could involve a biological agent. These concerns have been mostly forgotten today.

The push to resolve the open anthrax questions stemmed partly from the Agency's knowledge that al-Qa'ida had recruited the biochemist specifically to cultivate anthrax. Al-Qa'ida leaders were looking for a scientist who could build a program; the group's linkage to a Southeast Asian terror organization led to the identification of that scientist: Yazid Sufaat. Working near the al-Qa'ida heartland of Kandahar, in southern Afghanistan, Sufaat built a lab dedicated to the anthrax effort, only fleeing in the chaos after the 9/11 attacks.

The Agency WMD specialists slowly pieced together the anthrax picture, but a few questions haunted them, including the fundamental one of whether Sufaat had ever smuggled out anthrax samples that could be used in future attacks. For the Agency, those kinds of troubling unknowns motivated managers to press for continued detainee transfers to black sites, and for the authority to use enhanced interrogation techniques.

Among the prisoners transferred to the Program was a key player in the anthrax plot: Riduan Isomuddin, probably the most prominent al-Qa'ida-linked terrorist in Southeast Asia at the time of his capture and black site transfer in 2003. Known by CTC officers by the name Hambali, he was not only closely linked to the terror group in Indonesia that was connected to al-Qa'ida but he was also at the center of the Sufaat hunt, and he would become another of many the Agency pressed for answers about the confusing web of al-Qa'ida's global operations. The search for him had intensified in 2002, after the Southeast Asian terror group he masterminded, Jemaah Islamiyah, directed an attack against a nightclub in Bali that left 202 people dead. Hambali went on the run, but an operation in Thailand netted him traveling on a false passport in a town north of Bangkok. With his role as one of the most significant heads of an al-Qa'ida "franchise" operation—a regional terror group ideologically inspired by and in contact with al-Qa'ida leadership—he was a prime candidate for black site interrogation.

One of the first disrupted al-Qa'ida operations in America after the 9/11 attacks only fed the WMD concern, and the immediacy the CIA felt about how much time it had to question al-Qa'ida prisoners. Jose Padilla, an American who came in contact with al-Qa'ida in 2001–2, was arrested when he returned to Chicago in May 2002. He was under suspicion for involvement in several plots, including a "dirty bomb" that would disperse radiological material. Although there are questions today about how serious that radiological plot ever was, at the time the al-Qa'ida linkages with anthrax and Pakistani nuclear scientists were a concern, and the arrival of an American al-Qa'ida terrorist with possible WMD intentions was worrisome.

This single operation, the identification and arrest of Padilla, has become part of the disputed narrative of how harsh measures contributed to the CIA's successes against al-Qa'ida. Years later, the Senate Select Committee on Intelligence produced two detailed reports, one a majority opinion and the second from the Republican minority, offering dramatically different analyses of the effectiveness of the Program. Among the examples both cited: Abu Zubaydah's revelations about Jose Padilla. Quotes from the two documents highlight the debate about the utility of what Abu Zubaydah revealed. More important, these two snapshots begin to reveal the difficulty of judging the value of one detail in a vast sea of intelligence and whether the CIA could have accomplished its mission without it.

The Senate's majority report offers a blunt, damning assessment of the value of both Abu Zubaydah's comments on Padilla and the overall value of tough interrogations:

A review of CIA operational cables and other CIA records found that the use of the CIA's enhanced interrogation techniques played no role in the identification of "Jose Padilla" . . . . CIA records indicate that: (1) there was significant intelligence in CIA databases acquired prior to—and independently of—the CIA's Detention and Interrogation Program to fully identify Jose Padilla as a terrorist threat and to disrupt any terrorist plotting associated with him; (2) Abu Zubaydah provided information on the terrorist plotting of two individuals who proposed an idea to conduct a "Dirty Bomb" attack, but did not identify their true names; (3) Abu Zubaydah provided this information to FBI special agents who were using rapport-building techniques in April 2002, more than three months prior to the CIA's "use of DOJ-approved enhanced techniques. . . ."*

The CIA, though, viewed Abu Zubaydah's information as not only critical but a strong example of how the interrogation techniques had facilitated results. In its response to the Committee's analysis of Abu Zubaydah's reporting, the CIA stated:

> CIA believes the [Senate majority] Study overstates the value and clarity of reporting on Jose Padilla in CIA databases prior to Abu Zubaydah's debriefings. As it played out at the time, the combination of a suspicious traveler report and Abu Zubaydah's information allowed us to identify Padilla and the threat he posed. Abu Zubaydah revealed this information after having been subjected to sleep deprivation, which would be categorized as an enhanced interrogation technique after the program was officially underway.†

The CIA's response highlights the subtlety of intelligence analysis and the difficulty of evaluating detainee reporting in isolation. Agency analysts had received, prior to Abu Zubaydah's revelations, a report of a "possible illegal traveler" named Jose Padilla. Ten days later, Abu Zubaydah described a terrorist plot by individuals who, the CIA said, matched descriptions of Jose Padilla and another conspirator. Without Abu Zubaydah's com-

---

* Committee Study of the Central Intelligence Agency's Detention and Interrogation Program, pages 230–31.
† Examples of CIA Representations of the Value of Intelligence Acquired from Detainees, page 4.

ments, the CIA concluded, the Agency would have missed the importance of the earlier suspicious traveler report.

As if to underscore the complexity of evaluating detainee reports in isolation, another Senate intelligence report, this from the Republican minority on the committee, sided with the Agency.

This particular study's (the Committee's majority study's) claim gives the false impression that enhanced interrogation techniques played no role in obtaining important threat information about Jose Padilla during the interrogation of Abu Zubaydah on April 20–21, 2002, and implies that such information was really just the result of the "rapport-building" techniques used by the FBI that evening.

The CIA documentary record is clear that Abu Zubaydah was subjected to an extended period of sleep deprivation and other enhanced interrogation techniques during his interrogation between April 15, 2002, and April 21, 2002. Specifically, during this time period when FBI agents and CIA officers were working together in rotating, round-the-clock shifts, some of the interrogation techniques used on Abu Zubaydah included nudity, liquid diet, sensory deprivation, and extended sleep deprivation.

The sleep deprivation of Abu Zubaydah began on April 15, 2002. By April 19, 2002, Abu Zubaydah had been subjected to 76 straight hours of sleep deprivation in the form of intensive interrogation sessions and his ability to focus on questions and provide coherent answers appeared to be compromised to a point where sleep was required. Abu Zubaydah was allowed three hours of sleep at that time. On April 20, 2002, the FBI began its late-night interrogation shift at approximately 10:30 p.m. with Abu Zubaydah and continued until about 7:00 a.m. the next morning. During that shift, Abu Zubaydah was given a two-hour sleep break; time for prayer, food, and water, and a medical check-up. The CIA records indicate that by April 21, the day he identified Jose Padilla as a terrorist inside the United States, Abu Zubaydah had only been permitted 9.5 hours of sleep over a 136-hour period.[*]

No one at the Agency was thinking at the time of Abu Zubaydah's interrogation and how the utility of what he provided would be later debated. The ongoing war was too intense. Al-Qa'ida's advance on the ground, around the globe, seemed relentless, with attacks during 2002–3 in countries stretching from Indonesia to Saudi Arabia, Kenya, Turkey, and Morocco. These strikes included bombings against hotels and diplomatic facilities, beheadings of Americans, and strikes against Jewish sites, along with attempts against shipping, helicopters, and aircraft. It was just never clear where the next al-Qa'ida cell would crop up. Starting with the adoption of al-Qa'idist thinking by some extremists in the southern Philippines, the ideological influence of bin Ladin's globalist thinking—often deepened by direct personal links between al-Qa'ida leaders and like-minded leaders from other groups—also extended to South and Southeast Asia, the Arabian Peninsula, Africa, and then Europe. Jemaah Islamiyah in Indonesia, al-Shabaab in Somalia, al-Qa'ida affiliates in Saudi Arabia and Yemen, foreign fighters streaming into Iraq to fight the new American invasion, all

---

[*] Committee Study of the Central Intelligence Agency's Detention and Interrogation Program, Minority Views, pages 34–35.

erupted in the short years after 9/11. It seemed, at times, that al-Qa'ida was winning the battle for hearts and minds in areas where government reach was limited. Could Abu Zubaydah help crack the leadership structure behind this spread of the al-Qa'ida movement?

10

The Fateful Decisions

The Program grew and evolved in the field at least as rapidly as it did at headquarters, as interrogators learned what did and did not work on the detainees.

Early on, when headquarters executives and the field interrogators decided that Abu Zubaydah had shut down, they went to Tenet. His response, according to one participant in those conversations: "Let's figure something out. Get back to me." Less than a week later, CTC returned with options. They drove the conversation. Tenet didn't. "It's not that people didn't care," says one of Tenet's advisers from that period. "It [the Program] just emerged."

Tenet's management style, and particularly his personal relationships with managers in the Counterterrorism Center, helped shape the creation and oversight. Some senior officials who appear in the management chain of command between the director and CTC managers often were not included. It wasn't that the director mistrusted them; instead, with his personal style and engagement with individual managers several layers below him, he built a team unique to this operation. As he did with many of his decisions and actions, he did not rely solely on a CIA organizational chart to pick team members. "He was big on having focal points, belly buttons," remembers one of his most senior advisers. "This was totally countercultural."

The tone remained hard-hitting, occasionally too much so, some officers remembered. For example, well after Abu Zubaydah's interrogation, one CIA officer recalls a morning meeting about Khalid Shaykh Mohammed,* early in his detention. This prisoner had been found resistant to standard interrogation techniques, and was therefore undergoing their most aggressive, and controversial, option: waterboarding. One of the morning updates on the progress of these interrogations left at least one officer with a sense that there was an air of moral satisfaction in the room: too much "I'm glad we're working KSM" and not enough cool evenhandedness about the morally ambiguous path the Agency felt forced to take. This was not, though, a commonly voiced opinion among senior staff. The mood instead was grim, resolved, even occasionally rueful. "If nobody else will do it we will," many thought, a reflection on intelligence as the underside of foreign policymaking.

There was also, particularly early on, the persistent question of the motivations of personnel who were shifted to the Program. "There was a tendency to let people in who wanted to go," says one former senior operator from CTC, "rather than identifying the right people and asking them to go. It was attracting the wrong kind of people." Says another, "We needed more mea-

---

* Khalid Shaykh Mohammed (KSM), the principal architect of 9/11 and the most prominent detainee, was captured on March 1, 2003.

sured people." That lesson took time to learn, and the Center spent months, or longer, adding and then replacing staff.

As the Program developed, standard protocol for new interrogators required a psychological evaluation by the Agency's medical office. A few came back with "we do not recommend" comments from the office; they didn't go out. Says one manager who oversaw this process, "If they came in with an attitude of 'I can't wait to get my hands on these guys,' that was a red flag for us."

This was a real issue, especially considering how emotionally driven many were for a lengthy period of time after the attacks. In the midst of high-risk intelligence operations, calm decision-making was at a premium. Early on, a senior Agency operations official reacted to a perceived lack of cooperation by Khalid Shaykh Mohammed. "Get the biggest, baddest guys we have to make him talk," this official remembers hearing. As some of the interrogation team left the meeting, one asked how the team would respond to the outburst. "What are you going to do?" he asked one of the senior Program managers. "Nothing," came the response. "We can't do that." Over time in the Program, cooler heads continued to prevail.

After months of Abu Zubaydah's detention, in August 2002 the first interrogation team received the DoJ guidance allowing them to include tough interrogation tactics. The core team quickly realized that they had to gain more familiarity with applying the techniques. One interrogator remembers that they sought advice from entities that had used them in training, asking one of the US military services about safety precautions. They then designed the first safety policies with on-site doctors. And they waterboarded each other, for practice. To be clear: the SERE-trained psychologists never had authority about who was interrogated, or what techniques were authorized: they were contractors who followed orders, and they had no management roles. But they were crucial in helping the Agency understand the dynamics of interrogations.

The team had arrived at the first facility in mid-2002 to prepare, and they turned to developing the beginnings of what would become precise guidance about how to implement the techniques, and how they would coordinate during interrogations. Doctors, for example, advised what the prisoners should be fed, and they designed the waterboard. They continued to drill, practicing which positions each member of the team would be in during the interrogations, and how they would respond to an emergency. All of this was in the field, at the first site. Finally, an Agency official paid a visit. The memo from the relevant DoJ office—the Office of Legal Counsel—had come in. They were ready. DoJ was the final piece.

The memos provided the formal approvals; the on-site practice, and coordination, began to shift those memos from theory to practice. The Agency learned quickly how to interpret the black-and-white language so that it would apply to practical applications with real al-Qa'ida prisoners in the field. The memos from Justice came from the group responsible for interpreting the law for the Agency and translating law into guidance. That guidance was detailed, ranging from the techniques that were approved for the Agency to how those techniques might be applied.

Despite all this legal cover, and the detailed accompanying guidance, at least some participants still assumed that the ground would shift under them. Said one who participated in Abu Zubaydah's interrogation, "I specifically went to Catseye knowing that someday, opinions may shift. I nonetheless believed the Program was necessary, and that we Seniors [senior CIA officials, often referred to within the Agency as "Seniors"] could not ask subordinate officers to undertake an activity that we ourselves would not do."

The authorization for waterboarding included specific guidance. The technique involves the placement of the detainee on a board with his head angled down. With a cloth positioned over the detainee's face, the interrogator pours water over the cloth to simulate drowning. The written approval included mandates for the duration of each individual "pour" (how long the interrogator could pour water over the face of the prisoner, initially 20 to 40 seconds) and how long one waterboarding session could last (20 minutes).* Any officer on site was authorized and trained to say "stop" at any point in the interrogations, though some occasionally felt intimidated about doing so. Every team member was part of a group focused on pressing for answers from the detainees, and once the team agreed to an interrogation regimen, and the techniques they would use, a single member might feel awkward stepping in with an intervention suggesting that other team members had overstepped.

The interrogators judged, though, that this guidance translated into waterboarding sessions that were too long, and they reduced the duration of the pours. It was one example of how, over time, they were learning not only how to implement the guidance on interrogation techniques that had never been used

---

* These details, and the differences between "pours" and "sessions," help explain one of the disputes about how often prisoners were waterboarded. For example, some reports indicate that Khalid Shaykh Mohammed, one of the three detainees who were subjected to the technique, was waterboarded 183 times. Interrogators dispute that figure, arguing that KSM was never strapped to a waterboard for even close to that many sessions. They cite the gap between how many times water was poured over KSM during one session and the total number of sessions as an indication that critics of the program want to use numbers that make waterboarding appear to have been more brutally applied than they believe it was.

by them against hostile detainees but also how to use those techniques in combination. What worked? What didn't? And how would the mix change, from detainee to detainee?

Later Red Cross interviews of detainees after they had been released from CIA custody at the Guantanamo Bay detention facility, including Abu Zubaydah and Khalid Shaykh Mohammed, detailed their descriptions of these sessions.

Abu Zubaydah: "I was put on what looked like a hospital bed, and strapped down very tightly with belts. A black cloth was then placed over my face and the interrogators used a mineral water bottle to pour water on the cloth so that I could not breathe. After a few minutes the cloth was removed and the bed was rotated into an upright position. The pressure of the straps on my wounds caused severe pain. I vomited. The bed was then again lowered to a horizontal position and the same torture carried out with the black cloth over my face and the water poured on from a bottle. On this occasion my head was in a more backward, downwards position and the water was poured on for a longer time. I struggled without success to breathe. I thought I was going to die. I lost control of my urine. Since then I still lose control of my urine when under stress."

Khalid Shaykh Mohammed: "I would be strapped to a special bed, which can be rotated into a vertical position. A cloth would be placed over my face. Water was then poured onto the cloth by one of the guards so that I could not breathe. This obviously could only be done for one or two minutes at a time. The cloth was then removed and the bed was put into a vertical position. The whole process was then repeated during about 1 hour."

Underlying the evolution of how to apply the techniques was a basic philosophy used by the interrogation teams: learned helplessness. Everybody in the Program absorbed this philosophy, over time, from lower-level analysts to CIA senior managers. The phrase used to explain this goal, which was at the heart of every interrogation as the Program evolved, remains as memorably simple as it is controversial. The psychologists and the rest of the interrogation team would process each detainee and determine the level of the detainee's resistance; not all underwent harsh interrogations because some decided to cooperate early on. For those detainees who withheld information, the team would devise an interrogation strategy that started with relatively mild techniques—white noise, neutral food, and constant light were standard practice—and then escalated.

Learned helplessness, though, was only a shorthand for non-experts to understand the concept. It did not accurately capture everything the interrogation teams were trying to accomplish. The detainees weren't meant to be entirely helpless. They always had a way out of the interrogation process: they had the power to agree to talk. In a sense, a better description of the underpinnings of the Program might be learned dread, the same sort of dread many humans feel at certain moments in life. Some individuals, for example, will take long detours around bridges; they have a learned dread, a fear of heights that they have difficulty controlling, and they will go out of their way to avoid them. The interrogators thought they could apply this same concept to al-Qa'ida detainees by teaching them dread. The thought of returning to the harsh interrogation tactics would, over time, induce them to take steps to avoid the dark days already experienced.

The progression of walling, a common interrogation technique, underlines how the interrogators used the dread concept. The DoJ documentation describes the procedures as follows: "[walling] involves the use of a flexible, false wall . . . the interrogator pulls the individual forward and then quickly and firmly pushes the individual into the wall. It is the individual's shoulder blades that hit the wall. During this motion, the head and neck are supported with a rolled hood or towel." Interrogators didn't ask questions while they were using these techniques, and the popular perception that prisoners would say anything under duress wasn't the way they operated. For example, a prisoner might be waterboarded in the morning but not questioned until the afternoon, when the interrogators could pose a simple question: How does this named al-Qa'ida member [someone the detainee would know] communicate? If the prisoner didn't answer, the interrogator would then push him against the flexible wall. And then stop, and pose the question again. As one interrogator said, "There was no screaming, no Jack Bauer [referencing the popular TV series *24*]." It was more methodical than the movies, and far more calculated. There was always a plan for each detainee, and each session.

Over time, the detainee would associate walling, or the threat of walling, with fear. The tactic produced not only a physical response but a loud noise; the prisoners' eardrums would reverberate. Other techniques, such as an open-fingered hand slap to the face, weren't as effective in these interrogations because they couldn't be repeated over and over. "You can't do it [condition the prisoner] with a slap," said one interrogator, "because of the anger associated with that—it was an attention-getter, not a punishment, and you can't slap a person long enough to train them. You can't condition because you can't go on long." With walling, you could. Other techniques also fit this category. Sleep deprivation, for example, which was one of the most effective techniques the interrogators used. The interrogations didn't have to be violent to be effective.

The conditioning became more subtle as the detainee went through the process of associating techniques with dread. Over the course of weeks, an interrogator might place a collar around a prisoner's neck to create what was known as a "bridge," the psychological tool that the prisoner associated with walling. Later still, the collar might only sit on a table, or outside the room. "Are you going to answer questions today?" the interrogator might ask. The prisoner knew the consequences of noncompliance. Gradually, even the appearance of the collar outside the room would be sufficient conditioning. At this stage, prisoners would be considered "compliant," willing to answer questions without further coercion, even if they would never reveal everything they knew.

The detainees did not know the extent of the interrogation techniques, and they didn't know how long they might have to endure.* Was it a week? A month? The mental hall of mirrors they entered at the black sites contributed to the effectiveness the interrogators perceived. The unknown was a tool in itself: if the prisoner had known the limitations on the interrogators, the individual techniques might have been more easily defeated.

The exposure of the interrogation techniques, and the thinking behind the process, would undermine any future effort to remake the Program. Knowing the psychological mindset of the interrogators, the techniques, and the fact that the interrogations themselves had strict limits would allow any future terrorist group to prepare; in 2002 and beyond, though, they

---

* One reason some officers cooperated with the interviews for this book is that the interrogation techniques described here are already public, allowing any potential adversary to learn how to resist a similar suite of tactics. Because one of the core principles of the Program was the unknown—the detainees couldn't know what would happen to them, or for how long—the exposure of details about the Program, in the eyes of participants, undermines the prospect that future detainees would be susceptible to the same Program. They could train to resist it.

didn't know. And they couldn't prepare, at least not effectively. One senior executive who reviewed the Program says he had a columnar list of detainees that detailed what they said before and after they withstood EITs. "Two things jumped out," he says. "One is that it was effective. The second was that two techniques, waterboarding and sleep deprivation, jumped out as the most effective."

What the detainees did know, in their isolated world, was that life would not improve, and it might worsen over an unknown period of time, if they chose not to cooperate on some level. As the techniques escalated in harshness, the concept was simple: the detainee had to learn that there would be only one lifeline out; the prisoner could grab the lifeline or remain in the shadow world of coercive interrogations for a period that was never defined. The lifeline was the officers standing in front of him. Cooperation meant an immediate improvement in quality of life. Otherwise, the detainee learned, he was helpless to control the consequences. He loses track of time; he has no concept of where he is; he lacks a sense of when life will return to anything remotely resembling normal. He learns helplessness. And then he learns that the escape route is cooperation. The term Agency officers routinely used was *compliance*. Is this detainee compliant? Or is he withholding?

Part of the challenge interrogators faced was how to evaluate each detainee individually, trying to understand their level of resistance and their psychological state. These varied widely. One high-profile captive, for example, showed the same swagger at his capture that the Agency witnessed with many lower-profile captives. Some detainees simply assumed they would enter a US legal process and be assigned a defense attorney. In one case, when a defiant detainee, early in his detention, made this assumption, the Agency designed a one-time visual shock to shake him out of his comfort zone, quickly.

As he entered a black site facility, the detainee passed the solitary cell of another prisoner, Khalid Shaykh Mohammed, an icon for any al-Qa'ida member. Khalid Shaykh Mohammed, the architect of 9/11 and the anchor of al-Qa'ida terror operations, was called "Mukhtar" (the Brain) by some al-Qa'ida members. After his capture, one detainee told a CIA officer the loss of KSM had been "like the melting of an iceberg." During his early interrogation period, KSM was in the midst of a sleep deprivation cycle: when the new prisoner passed his cell, the cycle was underway, and KSM was hooded and shackled. The shock effect worked. The new prisoner went to his cell and curled into a fetal position. And he talked, says one interrogator who was there. Agency officers were convinced it was because he had seen Mohammed. First, he hadn't known of Mohammed's capture, and the fact that the CIA held him. Now he knew. Second, he witnessed an al-Qa'ida legend in a submissive position. The message was clear. You can try to resist, but not forever.

As a rule, prisoners were not allowed to mix. In one incident, a prisoner threw his food around his cell and refused to clean it up. Abu Zubaydah learned of the incident and "got pissed," remembers one Program manager. He was then allowed to enter the other prisoner's cell to clean it up, in silence.

In the report that followed the Red Cross meetings with former Program detainees, the International Committee of the Red Cross detailed what these prisoners said happened to them during the long periods of imprisonment, ranging from months in some cases to well over four years for the first detainee, Abu Zubaydah. Among those interviewed by the Red Cross were some of the most senior al-Qa'ida members CIA had ever apprehended, from Khalid Shaykh Mohammed to Nashiri, the architect of the bombing of the USS *Cole* in Yemen in 2000.

The accounts show that the prisoners did feel the sense of helplessness that the escalating series of interrogation tactics and the isolation at black sites were designed to create. The detainees spoke of their movement from facility to facility (some of their movements resulting from press leaks about facilities), without knowing where they were. They were always kept in isolation, with white noise and limited access to outside stimuli. As one officer later explained, "They could eat, sleep, talk to us, and masturbate. That's it." And the CIA tracked everything they did. Each cell was equipped with 24/7 video surveillance; the prisoners were never unobserved, some for years on end. Some of this was safety: the last thing the CIA wanted was a prisoner who succeeded in a suicide attempt at a secret prison.

The detainees complained to the Red Cross about their isolation and their disorientation and their inability to contact family. They were invisible men, not dead but lost in a secret detention system that was impenetrable from outside the Agency. No outsiders knew where they were or what they were undergoing. The prisons were, of course, designed to reinforce that lack of contact with the outside world; guards wore masks, to protect their identities, and the prisoners lacked access to newspapers, except when it might be a reward for compliance. Some reported later, for example, that after they had begun complying with the CIA's request for information their reward was current news; for others, it was sports news. This was another tiny inducement to cooperate, a step towards a sense of normalcy.

Small rewards, side by side with the interrogation techniques, were always part of the process of inducing the detainees to participate, even if they never fully cooperated. Better food or access to books, including copies of the Koran, for example, were standard rewards. Some would spend countless hours simply studying the Koran, looking for verses to reinforce their will to resist. They had continued access to the Koran, but they also now had the chance to devote time to other pursuits. The officials managing that first facility also wanted to diversify the detainees' reading material. They could make a lifestyle choice. And they did. Many improved their English in detention, and many debriefing sessions were in English, not Arabic.

The tight detention conditions meant isolation, too, for the CIA staff and contractors at the black sites. They were far from home, and the long days together in a sealed environment resulted in bonds between the seeming adversaries, captors and captives. Small things took on a relevance that seems unusual outside that closed world. Food, for example. One guard spoke to a visiting headquarters manager about a salmon meal the detainee was eating. Since the detainees were under 24/7 surveillance by cameras, they could communicate with guards by using signals to the cameras. In this case, the detainee gestured to the guard in what appeared to be gratitude and offered to share the meal with the guard. The guards weren't interrogators; the detainees might have felt that both were in a grim environment that they could not have imagined months or years before. "We were both just trying to get through it," was the explanation from one manager who visited several sites.

When they lived in such sparse environments, with so little diversion in their daily lives, small rewards took on oversized significance. Coffee was one. Food was another. Ensure, a nutrition drink, was the core of prisoners' diet early during their detention process. It provided the calories, vitamins, and nutrients they needed, but over time, it became increasingly more bland.* Food, then, was like the sports pages of a newspaper, and black site managers prepared special halal meals for detainees.

Khalid Shaykh Mohammed needed drugstore reading glasses; after cooperation, he got them. Another detainee had a prosthetic eye that was lost during his transfer between two black sites, so he wore an eye patch. The eye was located after a search, and he was thankful to learn that he could avoid the embarrassment of living without a false eye. At the most basic level, clothes could be a reward. In the early days of the Program, some prisoners were interrogated naked. Compliance could mean clothing.

The detainees had their own favorite rewards, some so small that they reinforced the concept of learned helplessness, where tiny glimmers of light are critical. For example, Snickers candy bars were a popular item among the prisoners. And for reading material? Other than the Koran, Arabic translations of the Harry Potter series became one of the most frequent requests.

The prisoners also received benefits unrelated to the rewards system, such as medical care that far surpassed anything they had been familiar with as al-Qa'ida members, who often operated in difficult environments without ready access to medical facilities. CIA officers, in those years after the Salt Pit debacle, were proud of the health care the Program detainees received. Agency officers often commented, wryly, that the detainees would later complain about their treatment at the black sites but that some of them had never received better medical care. The Agency offered a range of health services; there was even an optometrist

---

* As it turned out, the results of the dietary privations weren't all negative for the prisoners. Khalid Shaykh Mohammed was overweight at the time of his capture. Later, though, looking at himself in a government-issue sweatsuit, he declared that he "looked buff," according to one CIA official, who estimated that the prisoner had lost eighty pounds.

with security clearance who made glasses for detainees. Other prisoners entered the detention facility with major dental problems. They received dental care through the standard Agency practice: a dentist with a security clearance. Some of the later black sites had purpose-built exercise facilities, and in a sign of the kind of odd relationships that develop in tight quarters over long periods of time, the detainees and their captors sometimes used the facilities together and even played basketball together.

The interrogators came to understand how the interrogation philosophy played out in the minds of the detainees not only by how the detainees responded in the moment but also by what they later said, as they reflected on those early days. Abu Zubaydah offered interrogators an understanding of how he viewed the interrogation process and his ultimate decision to cooperate at some level. He talked about the interrogation techniques with one of the managers at the original black site. "You need to do this to all the brothers," he said, referring to his fellow al-Qa'ida members. "We have a duty to resist your questioning as long as we physically can," program managers remember him saying. "But everyone has a breaking point," he continued, "and when you reach that point, that's all that Allah asks. He recognizes that you're not superhuman. If you can take us to our breaking point, we will have fulfilled our religious duty, and then it is ok for us to be more open with you." Khalid Shaykh Mohammed talked, too, about how he needed justification to begin answering questions. One interrogator from that period had a simple interpretation. "They had to come to terms with the fact that they had done their duty," he thought.

Abu Zubaydah only spoke of this after his interrogation had reached a plateau during which he was compliant. There is a popular perception that the long years of their detention in CIA custody were a months-long or years-long history of unbro-

ken interrogation and harsh techniques. On the contrary, once
the detainees reached their breaking point, they typically didn't
turn back. Abu Zubaydah was a classic example: analysts and
interrogators thought he withheld secrets, until his transfer to
Guantanamo. But after the initial months of pushing him to his
limit, he became compliant. He got over his own psychological
bar and never returned to the resistance of his first weeks and
months. Like many detainees who followed, he came to believe
that they had done their duty to resist, and they moved on. Prisoners weren't asked intelligence questions while they were subjected to techniques. Instead, the techniques were used to push
the detainee to the limits of his resistance. Once he accepted that
there was no path but compliance, the questions might start.

As the Agency evaluated Abu Zubaydah's mixed responses,
and the truthfulness of them, some managers thought that analysts were too aggressive—sometimes to the point of arrogance—
in assessing what they were certain he should know. Whether
they knew it or not, this fed into the decision-making loop about
whether to continue subjecting Abu Zubaydah to the interrogation techniques. The managers at headquarters were more prone
to assume he was holding back, particularly early in the interrogation process; thousands of miles from interrogation sites, they
also didn't have to go through the on-site interrogators' face-to-
face realities. Some, or perhaps most, were not aware of what the
detainee was enduring at the black site. Over time, though, headquarters' assessments of detainee compliance synchronized with
black site officers' evaluation of the detainee. The interrogators
would judge when he had reached the point where he wouldn't
reveal more, regardless of whether headquarters specialists
judged that he was still holding back. Tough al-Qa'ida detainees
never revealed everything they knew, and interrogators weren't

going to take the steps to try to force them to, regardless of what headquarters said.

The headquarters assessments had an immediate impact in the field, where interrogators were with Abu Zubaydah every day, continuing the application of tough techniques. Interrogators pushed back on headquarters about continuing, and this strained relationship reflected the classic office divide that characterizes many centralized organizations: the distant management, in this case thousands of miles away, has the authority to direct and overrule the subordinate field office. Adding to the pressure on the CIA, senior administration officials in Washington were also pressing for answers about what Abu Zubaydah was saying.

The tension between CIA headquarters and the first black site reflected an imbalance between the two that would change over time. One of the architects of the Program, psychologist James Mitchell, later talked about his reaction to the headquarters directive to push Abu Zubaydah harder, with more waterboarding. Mitchell said he was among the interrogators who were "profoundly affected . . . some to the point of tears and choking up" when told by CIA headquarters to continue waterboarding. Mitchell said he did not believe interrogators needed to use the enhanced interrogation techniques to gain the additional intelligence Zubaydah had. Mitchell confirmed the accuracy of a *Washington Post* report that he and the other key psychologist, Bruce Jessen, were going to resign from the program after they were told to continue waterboarding Zubaydah, despite the fact that they said it was no longer necessary to do so.

Even as early as 2002–3, there was tension, too, within CTC. In particular, Center experts sometimes differed on how hard and long to press detainees when they did not appear to be revealing all they knew. Generally, the divide played out between two entities. The first, the al-Qa'ida department, known as "AQD," was the operational and analytic unit responsible for using CIA resources and working with partners to track and then capture al-Qa'ida terrorists. People-tracking was their specialty, using twenty-first-century communications tools, human sources, and support from other security services to locate terrorists across the al-Qa'ida network, and to coordinate captures. AQD specialized in knowing every detail about the activities of the terrorists in the al-Qa'ida network, but after the capture, a second entity in the Counterterrorism Center, the Special Missions Department, managed the rendition, detention, and interrogation of the prisoner. If AQD specialized in the prisoner's background, SMD's expertise was how to design an interrogation program to get the prisoner to talk, and to manage the detention black sites.

In general, CTC managers had simple lines, or at least they were supposed to. The AQD team tracked and caught the terrorists; the interrogators and SMD managed the rendition, detention, and interrogation. But the passion for the counterterrorism business, and the aggressive attitude AQD specialists had in hunting the al-Qa'ida target, led them to want more. On more than one occasion, the SMD specialists responded: We know the tolerances of these detainees. We think this detainee has reached his tolerance level. Sure, he might know more. We realize that. But we don't think he's going to give it up. With each detainee, CTC officers came to know that regardless of how compliant that detainee became, there were some areas, particularly related to bin Ladin, that the detainee would never give up.

The detention teams quickly understood that detainees' responses to the range of interrogation techniques differed. Some responded to the initial neutral probe—the first period of detention, when interrogators assessed whether a prisoner would provide intelligence without the application of tough techniques—but others were highly resilient. One Agency manager involved in oversight of the Program described these varying levels of resistance as a bell curve. In any group of individuals, some number—perhaps 10, 15, or 20 percent—would answer questions during the neutral probe; they didn't require tough interrogations. A large middle group would become compliant only after they withstood some period of harsh interrogation measures. At the other end of the bell curve, the far right end, a small number of the al-Qa'ida detainees were highly resistant, and a few would never really break.

Those differing responses among detainees meant that they didn't go through a standard, one-size-fits-all process based on what worked on any individual al-Qa'ida member. Many of the architects of the Program see the media portrayals of interrogation methods, particularly the depictions of CIA tactics, as suggesting that there was a mechanistic process for incoming detainees. This was not true. During the initial probe, to determine the detainee's willingness to speak, the interrogators would try to determine the detainee's resistance level; the process of developing interrogation options comes down to a relationship between the interrogators and the interrogated. Interrogators spend many hundreds of hours with detainees; one interrogator estimated that 5 percent or less of his time with detainees involved the application of interrogation techniques.

This is not to say that the relationship was pleasant, or that the interrogations lacked a brutal element. Over time, the interrogators did develop a policy mandating that they use the least coercive approach. Sleep deprivation, for example, was less coercive than waterboarding, and CIA policy required that an interrogator wouldn't proceed to that most aggressive tactic without going through a stepped-up process of less aggressive steps. As time went on, they could apply this suite of techniques more precisely, understanding which were more effective and which could be discarded. This policy wasn't always followed, but, headquarters and field officers fell into line as the Program matured.

The entire Program evolved quickly, and not only how policy and interrogations developed. The facilities, too, changed, as the Agency transitioned from makeshift compounds to the construction of purpose-built facilities for the growing population of detainees that eventually would number more than a hundred. Visitors to those facilities describe common features you might expect from a no-frills prison compound designed to keep prisoners in isolation. Later, all the facilities were sound-proofed. Other standard features—the individual cells, the nondescript nature of the facilities, the constant lighting and noise—often come up in descriptions by those who visited the facilities. But one additional feature also describes what they were like: clinical in nature, almost like medical facilities. And many remember the smell. Like a hospital. Antiseptic. "It was like Lysol," says one former senior Agency officer. Said another, "There was space for a bed, a pot to pee in . . . cement floors, a rack to sleep on."

His memories are consistent with the recollections of many officers who visited the sites. They remember grim facilities— not the grim of the movie *Zero Dark Thirty*. Instead, the interiors of these buildings were always clean, without natural light and with a prison professionalism that could seem oppressive. "The atmosphere was antiseptic, even surreal," said one CIA official.

For those who visited, the experience could be jarring.

There was at least one incident at a black site that demonstrated the difference between knowing the facts of what happened at those sites and seeing, firsthand, how the prisoners were treated. One senior Agency official visiting a site wept on seeing a shackled, hooded prisoner. That was not an unheardof response.

Other officers report facing the gravity of the interrogations themselves. Another former senior Agency official talked about the interrogation team's responses to some of the initial Abu Zubaydah interrogations at the Catseye facility. "You would think we would sit down afterward, as a group, to talk about the interrogation," he recalls. "But we all went our separate ways on the facility afterward." The sense, he reflects, was that the individual interrogation sessions were so intense and emotional that even trained participants who were regular team members required solitary time afterward to reflect and recover. While it might have seemed as such, it was never an antiseptic business. The team would then regather to go over the interrogation and plan for the next rounds, assessing what the detainee said, cabling details back to Washington, and calibrating the interrogation based on a judgment about the detainee's level of compliance.

The Agency's second compound after Catseye represented even more the rapid expansion of the program as al-Qa'ida takedowns accelerated. Detention managers initially envisioned one of the follow-on facilities with three prisoners; they soon had five, and then more, and they had to improvise. The planning was complicated, and logistics at the facility presented a few problems. The detention facility had in-house medical care, but emergency medical help was not nearby, a problem for both staff and what some detainee managers referred to as "guests." Finally, despite the Agency's requirement to minimize the number of local foreigners who were exposed to any part of the facility, managers there had to depend on local help for food preparation.

The growth was quick in coming. Not long after Abu Zubaydah's capture, the Agency faced another challenge, one of the early signs that the Americans and their allies were gaining momentum against al-Qa'ida fifteen months after 9/11: they closed in on another senior al-Qa'ida operator. The Program was on an upward trajectory.

11

Expansion and Training

In November 2002, one of the al-Qa'ida planners behind the attack on the USS *Cole* in Yemen was captured in the United Arab Emirates. Abd al-Rahim al-Nashiri was to be the second black site prisoner.

During the early stage of the Program, CIA managers greatly underestimated how the prisoner population might grow. In the months to follow, capture operations against al-Qa'ida leaders—widely viewed among CIA officers as easily the most important and effective operations, during those years, of all CIA successes against al-Qa'ida—moved far more quickly than CIA expected. Clearly, in the view of CTC managers, the Program would have to expand. And fast. And that growth couldn't hinge solely on makeover prisons built out of foreign-loaned facilities. The CIA needed prison facilities that it designed and constructed.

The Agency had to move from makeshift compounds designed on the fly for a few prisoners to new facilities for longer-term plans. "We didn't think business would be that good," said one of the senior managers of the detention program. Another remembers the Pentagon asking for help with its own detainee Program. The answer was no, partly because the Agency couldn't even handle detainees on the scale they were already managing.

The footprint of the new facilities was always small, even as the numbers grew. No other US government officials visited, and senior political leaders in Washington typically were not notified of the locations. Among all the secrets of the Program, the locations of those prisons remained among the most tightly protected facts, far more sensitive for Agency officers than the names of the detainees or the techniques. Exposing to the adversary what we are doing is bad enough, they all thought; exposing the risks our partners took, at our request, is simply too much. To help ensure security, CIA managers assured foreign partners that only CIA personnel would be permitted access to the sites. This held true during the duration of the Program, with the exception of FBI participation at the earliest stages of Abu Zubaydah's interrogation. Typically, knowledge about the facilities within the foreign security services that hosted them was also limited.

Many CIA employees, including senior managers, were aware of the black site locations, but most senior Agency managers never visited because such visits, especially a trip by a high-profile Agency official, entailed risk. Standard CIA offices overseas regularly hosted headquarters personnel who sought to take the pulse of their large overseas workforce. The black sites, though, were seen by Agency officials as a particularly sensitive matter, especially considering that they were not located at places Agency officials might otherwise visit. Keeping the profile low was always better. Even most staff in CTC didn't know where prisoners were held.

Prisoners tried to guess where they were, basing their judgments on tiny details. One of the most prominent detainees studied the packaging on food and liquids coming into his cell. From a water bottle, he thought he could determine the site's location. With a black site manager and a map in his cell, the detainee made his guess. "See the world," he asked. "I believe we are here," pointing to a country on the map. He was right.

Visits to the sites entailed consultation and preparation with local security services. Senior Agency travelers didn't just discuss operational cooperation with foreign security services. They built relationships over meals, cigars, personal gifts, and the one-on-one touch that only happens with face-to-face contacts. Few local security counterparts were even aware of the facilities and their purpose, though. There was a rhythm to the detainee debriefings and interrogations; outsiders might break the rhythm or bring scrutiny from local officials that could attract more attention than the Agency or its local partners wanted. The risk of outsiders became evident even in the most mundane circumstances. At one airstrip, local residents noticed air traffic. It was a CIA team, heading to a black site. Every detail counted as CIA headquarters dealt with logistical requirements.

Those CIA personnel who did visit occasionally met detainees, but they often didn't attempt to elicit intelligence from them. They used fake names to mask their identities, but their Agency affiliation wasn't necessarily masked; they sometimes were described to the detainees as senior Agency officials, to underline their importance. Some of the visitors' conversations with the detainees were just small talk, or even encouragement. One senior official, for example, told Abu Zubaydah that he was working to resolve the problem of long-term detention for the prisoners. It was the truth.

CIA officials also moved, when they could, to limit exposure for partner security services. When an early report surfaced in the media about one foreign location, CTC managers shifted prisoners quickly—within two weeks—despite not having a follow-on plan for prisoner transfers. It was another instance in which CIA officials took pride in their agility even as they critiqued media organizations that, in their view, seriously damaged not only America's relationships with allies but also efforts to fight the counterterror war. And central to that war, they judged, was the interrogation program.

As with any secret government program, code words and acronyms proliferated. RDG (Rendition and Detention Group) managed RDI: rendition, detention, and interrogation operations. EITs: Enhanced Interrogation Techniques. HVDs: High-Value Detainees, the al-Qa'ida members the CIA brought into its secret prisons, as opposed to mid- or lower-level detainees who also were sent to some facilities. Before they became HVDs, they might be HVTs: High-Value Targets. Any senior CIA official at that time would have instantly recognized any of these acronyms. Individual sites were each assigned a unique code name. Over time, though, many Agency officers routinely referred to the detention and interrogation program that would follow in classic bureaucratic shorthand. To insiders, Washington-speak about this broad range of CIA activities was reduced to two words: the Program. Almost everybody in the counterterrorism world at Langley understood those words.

With old lessons from Salt Pit and beyond in mind, CTC managers set about planning expansion in 2002–3. The third compound was significantly different from the first two: it was designed for twelve prisoners. As one manager of that time recalls, the Agency was hunting al-Qa'ida with increasing efficiency: "Business was getting good," he commented on the requirement to build more facilities with more holding space. It wasn't just the CIA operations that were progressing, though. Al-Qa'ida, too, kept up the pressure. In 2004 and 2005 there were the devastating strikes against transportation targets in Madrid, where 181 died, and London, where 52 were murdered. The London attacks were linked directly to the al-Qa'ida operators who had fled Afghanistan in the upheaval after the 9/11 attacks and then built a new safe haven in the unreachable tribal areas of western Pakistan. There was no reason to believe, even years after 9/11, that those same planners and trainers didn't have a reach into America.

Special Missions Department (SMD), the umbrella organization that oversaw the black sites, grew to match demand and became massive, by CIA standards.* In addition to the responsibilities for the detention and interrogation operation, the department also managed some of the Agency's teams that provided surveillance overseas. Not Hollywood style; some of their surveillance experts looked more like a local elder in an overseas capital than like James Bond. The department also helped manage CTC's technical operations—using high-tech tools to track terrorists. Finally, in one of the little-understood aspects of the explosion in global counterterrorism operations after 9/11, SMD managed counterterrorism coordination operations, centers the Agency created with foreign partners overseas. The variety of odds and ends under the group's umbrella offers a snapshot of one reason Program oversight wasn't always the top Agency priority; the facilities expanded quickly but the policies and procedures were slower to evolve: in the midst of a new war for the

---

* In the CTC organizational chart, a "Group" was subordinate to a "Department." The Renditions and Detention Group was under the umbrella of the Special Missions Department (SMD), which had a variety of diffuse responsibilities that did not fit neatly into other CTC departments.

Agency, the interrogation of al-Qa'ida prisoners was just one of a hundred priorities the bureaucracy learned to oversee.

The establishment of the SMD organizational structure coincided over time with the creation of a more formal training program for interrogation, designed to comply with the president's broad, initial directive, signed on September 17, 2001, that gave the CIA permission to hunt al-Qa'ida. (Formally known as a "Memorandum of Notification," the document gave the CIA the formal authorization for action against al-Qa'ida.) The formal training was also based on more specific guidance from the Department of Justice—the legal framework contained in DoJ's authorization for interrogations on August 1, 2002. With the rapid expansion in prisoner numbers, the Agency needed more interrogators, and training grew to hundreds of hours.

That training had a couple of basic components. Most immediately, headquarters had to build a group of certified interrogators. In November 2002, a few months after the issuance of the DoJ guidelines on enhanced interrogation techniques, CTC started formal training for individuals involved in interrogations. In mid-2003, another critical course began: debriefing training for individuals who were subject-matter experts, not interrogators. The debriefers were key in asking detailed questions after the tough early interrogations. Indeed, once the CIA judged that a detainee was compliant, subject-matter experts were vital in terms of extracting actionable information. They learned about Program goals, legal authorities, and the growing formal guidelines the Agency was issuing as the Program matured. Those formal policies and procedures were codified in a document issued in early 2003, "DCI [Director of Central Intelligence] Interrogation Guidelines," along with another DCI policy paper, "Guidelines on Confinement Conditions for CIA Detainees."

The Agency directed the interrogators and psychologists as

contractors—hired outside help and not staff—but also relied on them to advise on how to develop the Program. Many of the beginning stages of the Program were largely run by CIA staff, but its unanticipated growth and the fact that the Agency simply lacked expertise in interrogations fueled a demand for more specialists, and there weren't enough in the staff workforce to meet the requirement. The staff officers who were assigned typically weren't there long-term anyway. They signed on for tours of a couple of years and then moved on. To qualify as an interrogator, a trainee needed months of instruction in addition to on-the-job experience under a senior interrogator. None of the senior interrogators were CIA employees; all were contractors.

The contractors' role reflected more than the CIA's lack of expertise. The Agency also, with the demands of global deployments in the counterterror war, didn't have enough "core collectors"—trained field agents—to meet all its basic demands, and diverting those scarce officers to interrogation roles didn't make sense.

The staff expansion, like the management of the black sites themselves, came with headaches. The interrogation business was so critical, and so unique, that headquarters managers knew they needed a steadier stable of interrogators who wouldn't rotate off to other, more mainstream, jobs. An internal review in mid-2004 sharpened the issue, identifying the contractor/staff gap as a problem. Rather than pushing to increase the number of staff employees into jobs they weren't prepared for—and that would offer no career advancement for them—the managers of the detention and interrogation department moved in exactly the opposite direction. The senior specialists already on the job, principally the two contractor psychologists working under CTC guidance, then took on the responsibility of helping to train and certify the contractor cadre, always working under the direction of CTC staff managers. The interrogator role was not a career path for CIA officers. It was never meant to last forever.

As the contractors moved into the Program, staff managers at Langley had a sense that the boundaries between the contract interrogators and the staff officers responsible for managing and overseeing the Program had blurred. Staff officers felt compelled to reassert their authority, in the face of what they perceived to be too-aggressive contractor interference about how the Program should run. The contractors on the ground at black sites for lengthy periods of time saw problems they thought needed fixing, and fast. One longtime senior staff officer—who was responsible for training new interrogators—consistently pushed too far outside the lines drawn by DoJ. His training techniques, according to some, matched his field aggressiveness. He didn't respond well to headquarters guidance to change, and was removed from the Program during that early period of evolution.

The urgency behind the staff maturation wasn't solely internally generated. One story that reverberated throughout the CIA for years broke in 2004—prisoner abuse at Abu Ghraib prison in Iraq. Stories of widespread physical mistreatment at the facility, managed by the military, were bad enough; the problem was compounded for Americans with the release of graphic photos, including one widely reproduced image of a prisoner in a black hood standing spread-eagled on a small wooden platform.

The formal CIA Program never included a detention facility in Iraq. Nonetheless, the mistreatment of prisoners there sent shockwaves across the US government, and across America, and fueled trouble between the Pentagon, which had to deal with the fallout, and the CIA, which wanted to keep the Program as far away as possible from any confusion with Abu Ghraib. The Abu Ghraib scandal "changed the temperature" in endgame conversations, says one of the lawyers deeply involved in the negotiations. One participant characterizes the wrangling among agencies as a clear indication of the already existing toxicity in Washington at the time the explosive images leaked. "I got my own bags of shit," other agencies might say. "Why should I take yours?"

Program managers were not involved in prisoner facilities in Iraq, not just because the demands would have been administratively overwhelming, but also because the legal guidance for the CIA's detention of terrorists in the global counterterror war didn't cover Iraq. Legally, in other words, they could detain and interrogate al-Qa'ida prisoners. They just didn't have legal authority in the Iraq war zone, they judged, over prisoners who had no links to al-Qa'ida.

The Abu Ghraib scandal changed the landscape both at the political level in Washington and nationally, within various government bureaucracies. The Pentagon's long and painful acknowledgment of the scandal and its legacy fueled suspicions among senior Agency officials about whether Pentagon executives would want to expose more of the Agency's detention practices to deflect attention. From the Agency officers' perspective, this wasn't an idle concern. Regularly they would decline requests from senior Pentagon officials for more information about the Program. Field cooperation between Agency employees and the military, especially in Afghanistan, was excellent; Washington coordination was more fractious, over issues such as how the Agency could acquire more Pentagon-controlled drones for counterterrorism operations.

As a result, Agency officials responded to Pentagon requests with skepticism. There's no way the Department of Defense will ever run a covert program overseas that looks anything like this, so what lessons are they going to learn and apply from how CIA runs its black site facilities and interrogations? Over time, CIA senior officials grew to mistrust what they saw as Pentagon efforts to drag the CIA into the Abu Ghraib morass. One senior CIA official who briefed Defense officials in broad terms remembers facing repeated questions about the details of the Program. "I'm not authorized to discuss the Program," was his response, which was backed by the CIA's topmost executives.

Despite the haunting photos from Abu Ghraib, partner countries overseas continued to help. As the facilities and personnel expanded, the CIA also asked for, and received, support from a growing number of foreign security services that allowed the Agency to house prisoners in their countries. Some had faced attacks themselves, and they were deeply concerned about the growing al-Qa'ida threat not only of future acts of terror but of broader instability that might threaten governments.

CIA officials who spoke to some of those partner services during the middle part of the decade 2000–2010 say they were indeed supportive of operations that rendered their citizens to secret facilities. These foreign services knew they might receive intelligence from the interrogations of the al-Qa'ida prisoners. Further, because some of these security services faced such profound threats themselves, sometimes from al-Qa'ida or other extremists, they viewed the stepped-up CIA campaign, including the detention operations, as a sign of how serious the Agency now was in this joint fight. Said one former CIA executive, "Before 9/11, we'd ask our liaison partners to ask a bunch of questions that the al-Qa'ida guys wouldn't answer. We'd expect liaison to get answers." Now, these same liaison security services knew it was the CIA conducting the interrogations. It was the

CIA determining what to do when prisoners didn't cooperate. The closeness of the CIA's intelligence partnerships grew, across the globe, and the Program was just one small manifestation of the loose web of partnerships.

The need for cooperation remained critical because the number of facilities began to increase early on, and the CIA didn't want multiple sites in any one country. After the early and rapid inception of the detention and interrogation program was the process of institutionalizing the facilities. The first facility was altered specifically for the purpose it served, and overseen by the interrogation specialists who applied the techniques. Over time, facilities specialists and engineers from CIA headquarters got involved. They designed and altered facilities more to a one-size-fits-all standard than the highly personalized approach the on-site managers and interrogators at that first facility could take when they had only one or two detainees.

Participants still speak in sober terms about the Program, but this telling moment offers a window into the growing bureaucracy that came to surround an interrogation process that evolved from seat-of-the-pants operation to a large infrastructure. The interrogators needed more flexible walls for the interrogations. The walls were constructed of two pieces of plywood separated by a gap, similar to a hollow plywood wall. The noise and eardrum vibration a detainee felt when he was pushed against this artificial wall, his neck supported by a collar, served as one of the Program's most basic and most successful interrogation tactics. When a headquarters engineer built a new wall, though, he reinforced the interior hollow area with two-by-fours, eliminating the interrogators' ability to use it for its intended purpose of creating an echo effect. One interrogator remembers joining with a few colleagues to ram large sandbags against the wall to break it down so that it would be more flexible.

The steady flow of intelligence reporting increased as the Agency captured more and more detainees, and with that flood came unanticipated problems. For example, it dramatically increased the amount of reporting the CIA sent out to different US government intelligence agencies. With so much information streaming out of the black sites, there were issues in protecting the Program's secrecy. If a detainee spoke about how al-Qa'ida raised funds from donors across the Middle East, the Agency would be responsible for disseminating that information to other interested departments, such as the Department of the Treasury, State Department, the Pentagon, and the Department of Homeland Security. Analysts at those agencies would have their own questions about the validity of the information, and its source.

The Agency, though, was masking the origins of the reporting. No one in Langley wanted to confirm to a broad Washington audience that the CIA was holding prisoners such as Khalid Shayh Mohammed, so intelligence reports would simply make broad sourcing references—"This report is from a former senior al-Qa'ida member"—rather than using detainee names in reports. Even a regular reader of intelligence information inside the CIA's headquarters building wouldn't have a good sense of where the information came from. A report directly from a detainee—"raw" intelligence, in CIA jargon, or information directly from a source that hadn't been reviewed and put into context by experts—might simply cite an unnamed senior detainee as the source of the report, without identifying him, where he was captured, or his role. Broader analyses of al-Qa'ida—"finished" intelligence, or intelligence that had been looked at and analyzed by experts—used similar obscured references to detainee reporting.

This sourcing conundrum had a secondary impact on analysts at other agencies: because they didn't know which reports came from which detainees, they risked false corroboration. That is, they might use one detainee report to corroborate another detainee report, when in fact both reports came from the same detainee. There are ways to avoid this error—by calling the CIA and asking for clarification, for example—but the reporting mechanism was inefficient. This masking was a minor but persistent problem.

The effort to shield the program included CIA analyses that went to senior White House officials. Lower-level officials complained that the lack of specificity made the reporting harder to evaluate. But the most senior officials in the US government knew and supported the efforts. None of them wanted to risk detailed revelations about what everybody broadly knew. Senior al-Qa'ida members were being captured. Somebody in the US government was holding them. But don't ask questions and don't expect any answers.

Within a couple of years after 9/11, the al-Qa'ida apparatus was becoming better defined for CIA analysts. But so was the al-Qa'ida mindset, and a commitment from the group's leaders that offered an indication of why this would be a war that could last generations. Khalid Shaykh Muhammad, in one of his many explanations of al-Qa'ida leadership thinking, offered one dark picture that illuminated the long fight ahead. He explained how, in his view, al-Qa'ida leaders were men of peace. "Peace can only come when the world is converted, subjugated, or dead," he told one interrogator. "So our [al-Qa'ida] operations are accelerating our path to that day, and therefore bringing us closer to the day when we will be at peace." It sometimes seemed that it would be a war without end, now explained in the words of detainees who would never go home.

12

Maturation

With so many detainees in an expanding prison system, interrogators and analysts had a new opportunity to develop a terrorist think tank ("triple t"). Over time, they would experiment with how to ask the same questions of a group of detainees to see how they would respond, where they would differ, and which ones would appear to be withholding information. A selection of detainees all held in isolation and therefore unable to compare notes, for example, might be shown a photograph to identify. The photograph might have come from detainees captured in a recent raid, and the Agency might be looking to identify an unknown captive or find out more information on a prisoner they already were familiar with. The detainees might also take a step further, identifying al-Qa'ida members who might have known the new captive.

Among the little-known aspects of the history of black sites and al-Qa'ida detainees, the terrorist think tank ranks high.

Going from detainee to detainee, among those who were relatively cooperative, interrogators could quickly gather the tactical bits and pieces that are part of the core of terrorism intelligence. When they differed, it was a chance to ask why one detainee might be obscuring his knowledge and when they were similar, it was validation that the answers were accurate. There was no way the detainees could have prepared coordinated answers to the thousands of questions they would face after capture as the think tank gelled. Said one interrogator, talking about asking different detainees to interpret a coded message from al-Qa'ida, "They could give us a lie, but they couldn't all give us the same lie."

One of the efforts to plumb what detainees knew replicated what American school students wrestle with every day: homework. Overseers assigned bigger questions, ranging from the history of al-Qa'ida to the deeper ideological underpinnings of what they believed and why. In one of the thousand tiny details that black site managers had to think of, the detainees were given paper and pens to complete their homework. The pens, though, were potential weapons. So the Agency acquired flexible writing instruments.

The homework wasn't only intended to draw the detainees into revealing more about al-Qa'ida; it was also to keep them engaged, and to help them learn English that would aid in their interaction with the black site teams. Abu Zubaydah was the first recipient of CIA homework assignments. He, like a surprisingly large number of the al-Qa'ida detainees, spoke fair English at the time of his capture. As the Agency took more detainees, though, one reality surfaced: it would be easier to increase the English proficiency of the detainees than to train more CIA officers in Arabic. Further, for CIA officers who were trained to recruit informants and work with partner security services in war zones such as Iraq and Afghanistan, postings to black sites weren't ideal. The detainees started receiving more English-language books and movies in their cells, a change that had an unintended result. The Program shifted from detention to interrogation, from aggressive interrogations to less hostile questioning, and from questioning to a position the Agency didn't want to hold: long-term prison wardens.

The Agency had to develop policies and procedures to keep pace with their own learning curve. The memories of operations officers involved in managing the Program are consistent: the latter years of the Program were more disciplined, and better managed. For example, in contrast to the Salt Pit debacle in Afghanistan, a senior operations manager from the Counterterrorism Center remembers a vastly different Program in 2004, one in which policies and procedures had been mapped out clearly enough to squeeze out mistakes and instill discipline. During his tenure, one individual at a site stepped outside the boundaries of the interrogation protocols, "freelancing," in the language of CTC during those days. The freelancing wasn't extreme; the officer had improperly applied the approved techniques—in the words of the operations officer, "maybe putting a detainee in a stress position that didn't conform to what was prescribed." The interrogator was sent home. Even minor transgressions became unacceptable. In another overstep, an interrogator taped a detainee's elbows behind him and lifted him up.

The staffing procedures at the sites helped ensure adherence to policies, though even the overlapping staffing requirements didn't prevent occasional errors and abuses. To build redundant layers of oversight, for example, medical staff at the facilities witnessed all the interrogations. In an alteration to standard procedure at the CIA's overseas locations, these personnel had the authority to bypass the chief of station at the facility and communicate directly with the headquarters medical staff if they witnessed actions out of line with established procedures.

Even with all the learning and evolution, Program managers were dogged for years by the slowness in compiling a complete set of rules and regulations—along with the training and culture to implement a rule book—and the Program required tightening of loose policies and procedures. The new contractors who had joined to implement techniques inspired by SERE (Survival, Evasion, Resistance, and Escape)—and grounded in the DoJ guidance—had views that did not always accord with Agency staff personnel, and those differences emerged not long after the Program's inception. Some of the old-line Agency operators had their own independent ideas about what interrogation techniques should be, such as forcing prisoners into kneeling positions with broomsticks behind their bent knees. Nowhere in the DoJ guidance did such a technique appear. It wasn't lethal, or even more aggressive than other techniques. It was, however, unauthorized. "He said he'd learned it elsewhere," says one of the CIA managers involved in disciplining the operator. He was soon called back to the United States.

According to one participant at that time, the friction could grow intense between interrogators. It wasn't just guidance they were acting on, it was the interpretation of the law, and willful violation meant that interrogations were outside the law. When al-Qa'ida prisoners were transferred from the first black site to a second facility, a senior staff officer affiliated with the Program greeted them and the new interrogation team with a clear message: there's a new leader here. "Sit in a corner and shut the fuck up," was the message one member of the first team remembers. This was another manifestation of the "gloves are off" mentality that gripped some officers. In this case, the operations officer who took control of that second facility had prior experience with interrogations—in Central America, from the wars against Soviet influence years earlier.

Key Program participants have different views of the decision-making and oversight—who was responsible for some of the friction within the Program, for example—but they all agree that the Program's oversight was in transition not just during the first month or year, in 2002, but into the mid-2000s. Headquarters pushed to bring into line the new team members who had provided so much structure to the Program. One participant in the development of legal guidelines later characterized the initial legal guidance as "loose," even sometimes "sloppy," the result of a fast-moving bureaucracy that placed more emphasis on action than on perfection. Tight, persistent oversight from the Inspector General also led to tighter management in CTC. Counterterrorism officers came to view the Inspector General as an adversary, not an overseer, but they nonetheless felt compelled to respond to repeated IG reports about flaws in the Program. IG reports became a critical piece of Program evolution.

The Langley leash tightened, but not without adding discipline that stopped freelancing and closed gaps in field guidance from headquarters. In one instance, two officers who had been briefed on approved interrogation techniques decided they would interrogate one of the most senior detainees. One interrogator, an Arabic linguist who was not a trained interrogator, created an interrogation technique on the fly, a misstep that Agency officers still remember. Instilling fear was the motivation: he ran a power drill next to a detainee's ear while he was seated and blindfolded. Later, the same interrogator racked an unloaded handgun next to the detainee's ear. He never touched the detainee with either the drill or the weapon, but managers viewed these transgressions as extremely serious, and they still regret the early lack of sufficient oversight that allowed such events to occur.

The reaction to this event, though, illustrated the clear contrast to the Salt Pit era, and standard oversight practice designed for these situations played out in this case. When a security officer at the site learned of the violations, he reported them to a senior visiting CIA officer, who then notified CIA headquarters. Both individuals involved faced internal disciplinary action, and the CIA's deputy director for operations (the DDO, who oversaw all the Agency's spying operations overseas) then turned the cases over to the Department of Justice for review. The violations were severe enough that the DDO also requested an inspection of the black site Program by the Agency's independent Inspector General.

Interrogators themselves volunteered many of the abuses to CIA headquarters. There was a strong sense among them that some interrogators were going too far. One of them, psychologist James Mitchell, directly disputes reports that the psychologists were part of this overstepping; he and others say some black site personnel were clear in their opposition to headquarters pressure to push harder. "The Senate report [referring to the Senate's study in 2014 on the CIA's detention and interrogation program] leads the reader to infer that a lot of the concerns were expressed about me and Bruce, but it is often the case that Dr. Jessen and I were expressing concerns about dialing it back," Mitchell later said.

This calculus was simple. The Office of Legal Counsel at the Department of Justice provided the precise guidance for the conduct of interrogations. Nobody knew the ins and outs of how to implement the guidance better than the interrogators on the ground who were dealing with the prisoners and conducting interrogations frequently. When they saw some activity—sometimes conducted by individuals who were not certified as interrogators—that went outside the OLC guidelines, they reported it. Said one CTC manager who was assigned to the Center a few years after the creation of the Program and the early looseness, "It was disciplined." The push to standardize the Program was paying off.

The Agency was sensitive to the growing pains, and some CIA managers wanted a new look at this unusual intelligence operation to assess how it worked. In late 2003 to early 2004 Agency leadership commissioned the most significant internal review outside the Inspector General's studies, a study conducted by two long-time, respected Agency operations officers. Their mandate was relatively narrow: as Agency insiders, they were charged with looking at how the Program was managed, rather than making a top-to-bottom study that might include the results of the Program. Again, Agency leaders had a tempestuous relationship with the IG—one senior executive said he refused to meet the Inspector General without another official in the room—but the IG's pressure led to more oversight, and more questions. Said one participant in that review, "I thought the measures were understandable, with the exception of waterboarding." Even so, reflecting on the review years later—and on the intense criticism the Agency had withstood—he still went back to the pressures that led senior CIA executives to authorize the Program. "If [a future attack] worse than 9/11, I could see officers lining up to do this, maybe more."

All these reviews, from the after-action studies to the IG reports, resulted in a comprehensive rule book for all teams at black sites—interrogators, analysts, managers, security staff, linguists, and psychologists. They all had responsibilities for checks and balances as interrogations were underway. The Agency, and the teams on the ground, were well aware of the blowback should a detainee suffer life-threatening, or even mortal, injury as a result of interrogations. It wasn't only the on-site medical staff, then, who had the responsibility of calling a halt to any interrogation. Each participant had the authority to say "Stop."

One policy gap that represented the evolution of the Program involved the use of "conditioning techniques" that were not specifically authorized among the original ten enhanced interrogation techniques. Those methods including dousing prisoners with a water hose, for example, and flicking droplets of water onto a prisoner's face. Initially, those techniques were not considered a part of the technical guidance DoJ provided with the first legal memos, and the Agency had a written but unsigned (and therefore unofficial) agreement about what was appropriate outside the ten approved techniques. As legal teams changed at the Department of Justice, though, and as the Agency steadily worked to close gaps in its policies and procedures, the Agency lawyers realized they needed more formal, signed guidance, not just for clarity but also because DoJ indicated that the unsigned agreement didn't qualify as formal guidance. A review team within CIA, in response to a recommendation from the Inspector General, changed that, and the list of approved techniques increased from ten to thirteen.*

Along the way, there were also occasional disputes between CIA lawyers and operators about policy implementation. The lawyers became sticklers for conforming clearly to legal guide-

---

* The numbers can be confusing. As a result of the August 2002 written guidance from the Department of Justice, the CIA had ten authorized techniques, known as enhanced interrogation techniques. Interrogators, though, used additional techniques that were referred to as "standard," outside the EITs. Those "standard" techniques included dousing. As a result of this internal review, Agency managers combined the EITs with the "standard" techniques, resulting in a list of approved techniques that now totaled thirteen. Separately, the Agency had protocols referred to as "conditions of confinement" that outlined how prisoners could be held and isolated.

lines while the operators were learning to control their traditional CIA "We'll do what it takes" attitude. Legal guidance grew
and matured. Still, it took years to squeeze out minor transgressions. In one instance, a senior lawyer visiting a site noticed a
clear mistake. Music at detention sites was authorized formally
as a security measure, to ensure that detainees couldn't talk to
each other or hear what was going on elsewhere in the facility.
The lawyer returned from a site to report that one facility was
using music as a conditioning technique, to frustrate the prisoners. This was clearly a guideline violation. The music they were
playing? Children's songs.

Multiple motivations drove the never-ending push for tighter
controls and better management. First, there were the legal questions. CTC lawyers had to sign off not only on cables to the
black sites regarding how detainees were treated—whether the
use of interrogation techniques, for example, matched DoJ and
CIA guidance—but also the rendition of new al-Qa'ida prisoners
to the sites. According to one officer who provided legal counsel, some of the early cables were incomplete, and some applied
legal standards incorrectly. For example, the Agency applied two
foundational legal standards to prisoners who were under consideration for rendition. They had to be a member of or associated with a terror group (al-Qa'ida or its close affiliates), and
there had to be good intelligence that they posed a continuing,
serious threat. Those standards weren't being carefully applied in
every case. In some instances, said one observer, "It was just pure
sloppiness. The lawyers appeared to be too quickly saying to the
operators in the frenzy of those early years, 'I want to let you do
what you want to do,'" rather than slow or stop operations by
ensuring the operators had adequately documented the justification for operations.

Mistakes repeatedly accelerated the learning curve on legal

guidance and overall Program management. The transfer of a prisoner based on erroneous information shone a light on the criticality of matching close adherence to Agency guidelines with the aggressive push to move against al-Qa'ida among operators in the field and at headquarters. Khalid al-Masri* was picked up in 2003 and later transferred to CIA custody. "Within a few weeks," says one CTC manager who oversaw detention facilities, "we knew he was the wrong guy." After years of legal wrangling, the European Court of Human Rights awarded al-Masri 60,000 euros in compensation for a case of mistaken identity—a judgment against Macedonia, the location of al-Masri's capture. Again, the loose oversight of a controversial program came back to haunt the Agency. The lawyers, both within the Agency and at the Department of Justice, kept pushing for clearer controls.

Senior managers, meanwhile, gained knowledge about how to better manage detention facilities. In one case, several Agency officers point to a critical visit to the federal government's "Supermax" detention facility in Florence, Colorado, run by the Bureau of Prisons, where some of the government's most notorious prisoners are held in solitary confinement. One of the senior CIA managers who visited the facility remembers the visit as a key step in the Agency's maturing Program. "We completely redid training" as a result of the visit he remembers. And they did, expanding training to more than two hundred hours. In addition, the site tour offered Agency officials ideas about how to improve the design of their own black site prisons.

Other changes added depth to the Program. Training came to include the first female interrogators, for example. While they made critical additions to the teams for their endless commit-

---

* Khalid al-Masri was mistakenly detained by the CIA because his name is the same as that of a known member of al-Qa'ida.

ment and capabilities, they also brought something else: a psychological impact on prisoners who never used women in their own operations, and who were loath to interact with women as equals. "They [the female interrogators] alone will be an intimidation factor," the manager remembers thinking. One female interrogator became among the handful of the most pivotal operations officers in the CIA to oversee the Program. The psychological angle was only part of the story. Well before 9/11, CTC had developed a hardened cadre of female officers who were at the core of operations and analysis focused on bin Ladin and the emergent al-Qa'ida. Now, as the Program matured and the need for additional staff grew more urgent, female officers, some with a long history in counterterrorism, became key.

Just as the sophistication and duration of the Program led to an evolution in policies and procedures, the Counterterrorism Center's analysts' understanding of the value of detainee reporting evolved. Countless observers—critics of the Program and supporters alike—have debated the merit of reports from prisoners who often lied and who were coerced into talking. How can you trust an enemy forced to speak under duress? Such disputes, however, did not exist among analysts during the years of the Program. An adversary that the Agency had known largely from a distance, al-Qa'ida became a close-up reality, a group of terrorists about which the Agency now had firsthand knowledge. During those early years of mapping al-Qa'ida, the detainee interrogations were universally seen as an integral piece of the puzzle, but they weren't the sole source of information, nor were they more important than intercepts of al-Qa'ida communications or partnerships with foreign intelligence services.

The surprise about the "utility debate"—whether the interrogations produced useful intelligence—among these CIA officers centers on the essence of intelligence: How can an analyst judge whether a detainee, especially one who's likely to lie under duress, provided anything of value? Why do you believe detainees who lie? Says one former CTC operator who questions some of the Program implementation, "We tried to be nice and got nothing. My own personal experience is that the Program worked. We got the data. He [the detainee] doesn't say he's [an al-Qa'ida target] at 31 Elm Street. That's not how it works. I don't understand the utility debate."

The hunt for bin Ladin was always an interrogation subject, but it would be misleading to believe that it was at the heart of the vast majority of questions the detainees faced. Interrogators knew that detainees had their limits. They would be forthcoming with some information, over time, especially historical data that they thought was not particularly valuable. At the other end of the spectrum, though, was information that they might die to protect. "If he has stuff in his head he's not willing to give up," says one interrogator, "then he's willing to die for it." Detainees weren't ever viewed as fully cooperative; they would never reveal all. It was the bits and pieces, not the huge breakthroughs, that made the Program a central feature in the Agency's growing body of knowledge about the enemy.

This isn't to say that interrogators ignored the most important questions. The hunt for bin Ladin was part of the standard questioning for any detainee. And there were typical categories of questions any expert would want answers to. First, there was threat: before anything else, is there information somewhere that might help stop an imminent attack? Then the questions transitioned to locational information: what does the detainee know that might help identify other individuals or cells? Over time, the questions might become highly tactical: who is this in the photo you're looking at? What is the email address for this individual?

For some detainees, interrogators flipped questions. Rather than asking what they knew about a specific bit of information or individual, the interrogators might ask a compliant detainee to create his own questions: if you were looking for this person, how might you find him?

The detainee interrogation process differed fundamentally from an interrogation during which the endgame would be a prisoner's confession. One former senior CTC manager points to the argument that prisoners, under harsh interrogation, will confess to anything to escape the interrogation cycle. Interrogators weren't looking for confessions; attempts to equate intelligence interrogations with law enforcement questioning of a suspect fail to address this fundamental distinction.

A confession by a criminal might mark the end of the case. For the Agency, what the detainees admitted marked the beginning. When they started talking, the CIA used what they said to begin taking apart an al-Qa'ida operation or an al-Qa'ida cell. Assigning guilt to the detainee was irrelevant; the information was only valuable if, pieced together with other information, it allowed intelligence analysts to understand al-Qa'ida more clearly. It wasn't enough for a detainee to confess. He had to provide information that corresponded to other intelligence well enough for the Agency to more deeply understand al-Qa'ida.

A dynamic among interrogation teams also developed. The interrogators and psychologists were specialists in the process, but they were not experts steeped in al-Qa'ida. That was the analysts' job, and they turned out to be critical in the teamwork that resulted in the individual interrogation plans. The reason was simple: to understand when a detainee is lying, the interrogation needed to start with baseline knowledge about the detainee. Where had he traveled to? Whom had he met? What activities had he been involved in? Given his stature and position within al-Qa'ida, what should he reasonably know?

Understanding details about top terrorists allowed the teams, with the analysts' help, to fashion questions that would determine the detainee's level of compliance. If, for example, a terrorist lied repeatedly about his travel over time, the team could conclude that he should not graduate from the intense stage of the interrogation process that included harsh techniques. "Why are they omitting things?" asked one senior operator, reflecting on criticisms that detainees under pressure would lie. "Why are they letting other things go? If a detainee downplays the role of somebody he knows, what am I missing?" This wasn't, after all, the Agency's first experience with lies. "Even double-agent cases tell you certain things you didn't know before," said the same operator, with decades of experience working against Soviet bloc security services. Said another manager, "If you don't think you can deal productively with sources who lie, don't have a CIA."

A revolution in intelligence analysis accelerated in the years before 9/11, feeding the pool of analysts who provided this tactical level of expertise about individual al-Qa'ida members. Traditional analysts specialized in basic areas—politics, economics, military affairs, and weapons proliferation, for example. A new breed, though, grew along with the explosion in digital data, from cellphones to email to social media. Those analysts started using specialized data analysis techniques to understand not broad trends, such as wars or political change, but the activities of specific individuals. For example, one of this newer generation of analysts might focus on one terrorist, trying to understand everything that terrorist did. Travel. Communication. Money. Every move. The terrorist was the analyst's target. And the new analyst had a new name in the old world of intelligence: the targeteer.

Targeteers in the counterterrorism world continued to build a new analytic tradecraft, understanding what was called the "pattern of life" of a specific individual, such as a senior al-Qa'ida operations coordinator or a lower-level courier. That analyst would follow every bit and byte of data US intelligence agencies could collect about that individual, using new tools that hadn't existed before the 1990s and that grew quickly in sophistication during the twenty-first century. Data analysis that allowed headquarters analysts to integrate vast troves of information; hard-drive exploitation from captured laptops; and penetration of the new global communications networks were new, and critical. Using these tools, coupled with just simple, grueling research, helped analysts develop a fine-grained knowledge of the patterns of life of high-profile al-Qa'ida members, knowledge that allowed the teams to box in detainees. The team might start with questions where the Agency analyst knew the answer but the detainee wasn't sure how much the Agency had collected. As the detainee lost confidence about his understanding of what Agency specialists knew and what they didn't, the team might insert tougher questions. They avoided yes/no questions, instead giving the detainees a chance to comply, or to spin a tale that the targeting analyst would know was false. During those questions, if the Agency knew enough about the detainee, the message was clear. One interrogator described the undercurrent of the interrogations: "You can't hide. We know who you are and what you've done."

The targeteer role for analysts didn't come without downsides. Analytic managers obviously had no experience in sending analysts out to interrogation facilities to participate in detainee interrogations that might expose them to jarring images of hooded, shackled al-Qa'ida detainees. The analysts were vol-

unteers, not interrogators, so CTC developed a small training program for them. Over time, their role became critical in
the teams that designed individualized interrogation days for
each detainee. The interrogations were scripted by groups that
included targeteers along with black site managers, psychologists, interrogation experts, and medical personnel. The design
of the interrogations themselves hinged on two basic elements.
First, which techniques might work for a detainee, based on a
graduated approach. And second, what should the detainee be
expected to know, based on an expert analyst's understanding of
the detainee's history, background, and role in al-Qa'ida.

As the learning curve for both operators and analysts grew, the
Program drew increasing attention from both inside and outside
the Agency. One key turning point centered on the capture of
a lower-level detainee who had been transferred to one of the
black sites in the spring of 2003. Despite his modest status in
al-Qa'ida, this detainee was one of many second-tier al-Qa'ida
targets who were sent for interrogations. In his case, though,
the interrogation techniques were off the table because of an
impasse: the CIA was awaiting further guidance on the legality
of the EITs, and the Department of Justice didn't always supply the necessary legal judgments (on paper) very quickly. The
White House knew it, and the battle was on. He would be interviewed at the black site. He would not, though, be subject to the
harsh interrogation techniques.

The detainee's transfer gave the CIA's demands a sense of
urgency because the question of whether DoJ would retract its
steadfast legal backing for the Program now shifted from theory
to reality. Without the Department's judgment on paper, CIA
officials from the director down drew a line in the sand on this

one prisoner. The message was simple: the Agency won't proceed with techniques without a written opinion from DoJ defining its position. The answer to the legal limbo from senior Agency officials, including the director, was crystal clear: no paper, no Program. When Justice backed away from clarifying their opinions in writing, Agency leaders played their hand. They temporarily shut down the Program in 2003. Prisons stayed open, but the interrogation techniques stopped.

Given the seriousness of the legal issue, and the still nagging view that the government had to do everything in its power to prevent another attack, it was inevitable that the White House stepped in. The attorney general, John Ashcroft, was not only a political appointee, he was a political player. For the Agency to press him to close out the work on the legal paper—which everyone knew would go public some day, with repercussions no one could predict—the White House would need to push. Reluctantly, Justice heavyweights came to the table, with senior White House officials, to talk.

The hiatus in interrogations, and the nasty debate about this one detainee, also brought to light another issue. Time was ticking and, in the words of one CIA executive working directly with DoJ counterparts, "They [DoJ] wiggled." Some in the White House thought the Agency was becoming overly legalistic in its refusal to reverse the hiatus in interrogations, and the White House meetings were tense. As the debate over demanding more specific DoJ guidance continued, one senior White House official looked at the CIA team during a particularly heated meeting. "If anything happens," this Administration official said during an interagency meeting about reinstituting interrogations, "it's on you."

These legal debates about the permissibility and latitude of the Program included a phrase that began with lawyers but spread throughout the group of operators who managed the Program. The phrase, "shock the conscience," was drawn from the Fifth Amendment, which prohibits government conduct that is intended to injure a prisoner in some unjustifiable way. In DoJ's newly drafted opinion, the CIA's techniques didn't meet this criterion; the DoJ memorandum judged them "reasonable," given the grave national threat. Further, the memorandum read, the CIA's techniques were designed to minimize serious long-term physical or psychological risk to the detainees.

The interpretations that followed the 2003 debate led Agency officials to restore the Program; harsh interrogations would begin again. But the days of blanket approvals for the CIA were already over, another clear sign that the interrogations were losing unambiguous support. Going forward, approvals for individual interrogation techniques would be case-by-case: the "shock the conscience" standard meant the Agency would have to use a sliding scale to determine which detainees reached the level of triggering individual EITs.

During his tenure, Tenet had always sought, repeatedly, greater clarity about the soundness of DoJ's opinions, especially as department leaders seemed to slip in their once stolid legal backing for the Program. A Washington insider, after years working as a congressional staffer, understood the importance of backing the zealous support the Agency received in the early years with formal documentation. His immediate successors, long-term congressman Porter Goss and retired general Michael Hayden, took their own steps to affirm that the program was on solid ground. Some of their efforts differed from Tenet's in one simple respect: Tenet had been there from the start, before and after 9/11. He knew the genesis of the Program, and who knew what the detainees had said and how counterterrorism officials viewed the criticality of the picture the detainees' provided of the hazy al-Qa'ida adversary. These new directors didn't have that history. Their challenges, too, were different: they needed to assure themselves of the Program's efficacy because the Washington political landscape was shifting, and probing, public questions about the Program were on the rise. They would be the ones to defend it. First, though, they needed to understand it.

They were spurred not only by these swirling external questions but also by intense scrutiny coming from inside, resulting in some of the most contentious internal battles of the time. The Inspector General has a unique role in the Agency, and at other federal agencies with equivalent positions. The post was created to provide an oversight mechanism at agencies that would be outside normal management chains—in other words, outside agency and department heads' capability to influence the outcome of a potentially embarrassing internal investigation. Inspectors General answer to Congress, without having to clear their findings with the entity they are inspecting. If the IG at the Agency found problems in something the CIA was doing, the CIA director couldn't stop the probe, or stop the IG from presenting tough findings to Congress. Nowhere in the Agency's recent history was this unique IG power and authority more evident than in the IG's investigations of the Program.

Through the years of the Program, the Inspector General continued to be a lightning rod within the Counterterrorism Center and outside, up through the Agency's management ranks and into the seventh-floor executive suites. The level of suspicion between CTC and the IG was somewhere between high and feverish, and the temperature would remain high during the entirety of the Program. The reasons weren't complicated.

The relationship between Agency executives, including those in CTC, and the Inspector General's office was tense even before the investigations into the Program. In retrospect, there was little chance that the back-and-forth between the IG and various executives in the Agency, from multiple CIA directors down to CTC leaders, would ever lead to a healthy dialogue. In a formal assessment of the Counterterrorism Center immediately before 9/11, the Inspector General's office had found CTC to be "well managed" and successful in carrying out the Agency's "counterterrorism responsibilities." A few years later, the IG's after-action on the CIA's performance surrounding the 9/11 attacks was blistering, referring to the Center's focus as primarily "tactical" and "operational" and lacking in strategic direction, and tough on the performance of Director Tenet's leadership on counterterrorism. The response from Tenet and CTC managers was a series of no-holds-barred rebuttals. Tenet responded that the IG had "mischaracterized" his leadership; CTC managers signed a response to the IG that referred to "significant" misrepresentations in the IG report and called the conclusions "unreal." Hardly a series of exchanges that would allow for a reasoned discussion of views on the explosive operation that was the Program.

That, however, wasn't even the low point. The IG also engaged in a lengthy back-and-forth with a succession of CIA directors about the accountability of specific employees for what the IG judged as performance failures before 9/11. The standard process for considering disciplinary action in the case of such allegations would be a formal accountability board, a group convened to determine whether employees guilty of significant performance lapses should receive penalties such as letters of reprimand or even removal from service. These boards were rare at the Agency, and the universal view of CIA staff at every level was that disciplining individual officers would suggest they were accountable for what was a government-wide failure to confront al-Qa'ida before 9/11. The mood on this issue was tense, even vitriolic.

Counterterrorism managers and Agency leaders developed a deep-seated mistrust of this unique oversight mechanism that went far beyond the usual questions. The IG's responsibility wasn't to find where the Agency was performing well; it was to point out weaknesses, including poor management. The Agency managers who dealt with the IG during that period believe, uniformly, that this unique oversight mechanism broke down.

On the top of these bruising exchanges about the pre-9/11 assessments came a series of IG studies about the Program itself. The IG's oversight was a watershed in both Program management and in attitudes about what the Agency was doing. The inspection reports mixed in with other questions across Washington in the summer of 2004, offering sometimes painful perspectives about what the CIA was doing, whether it complied with the DoJ guidance, and whether the Program was sustainable over the long term.

The IG report (issued in 2004 under the innocuous title "Counterterrorism Detention and Interrogation Activities") cited management oversights and "deviations from approved procedures," later declassified with extensive redactions. "Agency efforts to provide systematic, clear, and timely guidance . . . was inadequate but improved considerably during the life of the Program as problems have been identified and addressed," it also stated, mirroring the recollections of many Program managers about the rough early period in the Program's evolution.

The IG pointed out examples of the deviations, another indication that interrogators had overstepped their authorized boundaries before the Agency issued stricter guidance and oversight rules for the Program. "An experienced Agency interrogator reported that the . . . interrogators threatened Khalid Shaykh Muhammad. . . . According to this interrogator [unidentified in the IG report], the . . . interrogators said to Khalid Shaykh Muhammad that if anything happens in the United States [referring to al-Qa'ida terror attacks], 'We're going to kill your children.'" In another overstep, about September 2002, the report says an individual reported that a debriefer had staged a mock execution. The report goes on: "[Name redacted] was not present but understood it went badly; it was transparently a ruse and no benefit was derived from it. [Name redacted] observed that there is a need to be creative as long as it is not considered torture." The report then goes on to offer a sample of how the rules changed. "[Name redacted] stated that if such a proposal were made now, it would involve a great deal of consultation. It would begin with . . . management and would include CTC/ Legal. . . ."* Notably, Program insiders point out that it was their own personnel who identified some of these problems, including this mistake.

Counterterrorism officials' views of the IG went beyond standard suspicions, though; the relationship had already been poisonous, as CTC officers felt they were under scrutiny for too long, across too many fronts. In addition to the IG inspections, the 9/11 Commission blistered the Agency for some of its performance before 9/11. The WMD commission (the Commission on the Intelligence Capabilities of the United States Regarding Weapons of Mass Destruction, established in February 2004], coming in the wake of the revelations that the CIA's collection and analysis about Saddam Hussein's special weapons programs were seriously flawed, created an atmosphere of us-versus-

---

* The ellipses represent redactions of words or phrases in the declassified IG report.

them. From the Agency's perspective, they were clawing their way through a tough fight against al-Qa'ida while facing attacks from various fronts—the Congress, the media, and the Inspector General.

Underlying their already profound suspicions was the overwhelming view that the Inspector General was personally opposed to the Program on ethical grounds and that his views colored the work of the entire IG workforce and the inspection documents they produced.

John Helgerson, the inspector general during that period, was a well-respected senior executive in the Agency with a long history of senior analytic assignments and a reputation as a stoic, even-tempered leader. He also had a well-known aversion to the Program, according to Agency officials who were at the receiving end of his reports. His office was the only element of the Agency where this kind of deep-seated opposition was evident. As a result, operations managers in the Center had a clear interpretation of the IG's opposition: he couldn't conduct unbiased investigations, in their view, of activities that he so clearly saw as not only repugnant but morally unacceptable. The animosity between the IG and CIA managers working counterterrorism issues, including CIA directors, never cooled.

CIA director Porter Goss was confirmed for the position in September 2004, and he immediately faced one of the key problems that fed the tensions with the IG. That year, the IG had conducted a study of the Agency's pre-9/11 performance against al-Qa'ida, and that study included names of CIA officers, some in relatively junior positions, who were identified as not having performed in a "satisfactory manner." Inside the Agency, this finding in the IG report was explosive: if the Agency chose to release the names of individuals cited, CTC officers believed those individuals would be seen as personally responsible for a national failure to confront al-Qa'ida that led to 9/11. Goss inherited the study and the question: should he release the names?

Goss came to the Agency with a solid reputation as chairman of the House of Representatives committee that oversees intelligence, but he got off to a difficult start and never recovered. He had been a CIA officer in the 1960s, so he brought an understanding of the intelligence business, but he also brought a cadre of staff who were buffers between him and even senior executives, and the abrasive style of those staff doomed his tenure. Bespectacled, soft-spoken, courteous, almost courtly in manner, he was hard not to like. But his distance from the day-to-day business—CIA directors before and after were known for their tactical involvement in CIA operations, especially counterterrorism—and his unwillingness or inability to rein in the newcomers who came with him undercut his authority.

On the issue of the IG report and issuance of the names, though, Goss stood firm. CTC's view was clear during the terms of Tenet, Goss, and Hayden. First, the most senior managers argued that the IG should hold them responsible for shortcomings in the pre-9/11 era. They were trying to shield their subordinates, but their arguments didn't hold water in the IG's office. Finally, the issue went to the Agency's executive suites. And the question of naming CIA officers found its way to the director's desk. The officers named in the report had been notified that their fate—whether the American public would see their names associated with a report that said the Agency made mistakes in the lead-up to 9/11—was about to be decided. Few, if any, of them thought the Agency would protect them. They still believed in the counterterrorism mission, but they were highly skeptical that the snake pit of Washington bureaucracies, or the CIA itself, would offer any protection.

The IG wasn't the only outside entity questioning the Program. A series of officials at the Department of Justice began their own reviews of those initial memos that had served as the foundation for the interrogation process in mid-2002. Almost inevitably, from multiple corners—the media, the IG, the Department of Justice, and the CIA officers overseeing prisoners who had now been in custody for years—the long-term viability of the Program was coming into question. What had started as a clandestine operation conceived in the heat of post-attack Washington was now transitioning to the stage every senior CIA officer had always anticipated. The controversy about the Program and what the CIA had done to prisoners was escalating. The Program was no longer a secret.

Officials have varying recollections of how long Washington was comfortable with a blank check for CIA counterterrorism operations. Two years? Three years? One senior manager has clear recollections about the transition in Washington attitudes that he witnessed: "I started to feel that we were losing support maybe in 2004. Politicians took over." The lead-up to the Iraq war had eroded national unity, and Congress's relationship with the White House and the CIA, and Abu Ghraib transformed what had been a post-attack period of steel will across the country into questions about how American values played out on the battlefield. At one of the most critical CIA field stations, the pace of operations against al-Qa'ida players remained high. Then, in about 2005, one senior field manager had one of those game-changing moments. That field office, at the center of the fight, picked up another senior al-Qa'ida player.

This time, the direction from headquarters was different, the tone was new. Field office managers read the directive aloud at a staff meeting. "Make sure the detainee gets eight hours of sleep," one field manager says he read at an office meeting in a country where some of the detainees had been captured. The response across the office was simple. "Nobody in *our* office gets this much sleep," echoing the same reaction others had. It wasn't the specific guidance that raised eyebrows. It was the change in direction and the souring mood. The world was moving on from 9/11; Agency headquarters was becoming more sensitive to risk. And there was nowhere that the growing chill was felt more than in the Program.

13

The Program Goes Public

From Abu Zubaydah to Khalid Shaykh Muhammad and dozens of others, key al-Qa'ida players began disappearing after capture, lost in the web of secret prisons. Despite their prominence, few questions arose publicly about what had happened to them. Media scrutiny during the early years of the Program cropped up periodically, but media requests for information were not intensive. Red Cross demands, though, came regularly. The ICRC made its first written request to the CIA for more information as early as 2002, with subsequent requests in 2004 and 2006. The detainees had entered no known judicial process, and nobody acknowledged holding them after they disappeared. The governments that had handed them over declined comment. The Red Cross knew they had to be held somewhere, and the CIA was obviously the answer. But there was no way the Agency could acknowledge the program without blowing the lid off it. The

CIA eventually built a relationship, surprisingly, with the Red Cross. And continued to decline comment on media requests.

Then, as early as 2003, the *New York Times* began to report the shadowy outlines of the Program. At that time, the Department of Defense also detained captives, and the *Times* covered the detention of former Iraqi president Saddam Hussein in an article that also touched on the CIA's detention facilities. The two programs were entirely separate, but the story generally discussed the evolution of America's detention of prisoners in the post-9/11 era.

"The CIA has established its own detention system to handle especially important prisoners," the reporters wrote, going on to refer to the Agency's first high-value detainees, Abu Zubaydah and Ramzi bin al-Shibh.* The coverage also, though, referred to one specific country that hosted the first black site. The same reporters also started to open the door on interrogation techniques, writing of sleep deprivation as a Pentagon practice for some prisoners. Little more than a year after Abu Zubaydah's shift to a secure location managed by the CIA, the curtain of secrecy was slowly lifting.

The *Times*'s coverage also opened the door on the detainee story. Not the press coverage of all US government detainees—the Abu Ghraib scandal from Iraq, for example, led to massive coverage by US media—but instead the far narrower story of what had happened to the high-level figures that had gone down in global raids and then disappeared. That leak, though, wasn't fatal. In the early years, perhaps as a sign of the national unity

---

* Of the hundred-plus detainees the CIA processed through various black sites, one senior manager who oversaw the Program estimates that perhaps fifteen were top-tier al-Qa'ida operators, or true HVTs.

that followed the 9/11 attacks, the Agency's press office faced few—surprisingly few—inquiries about what had happened to these phantom prisoners. One former senior Agency officer involved in media relations speculates that the media might simply have assumed that the CIA would decline any requests for information.

The reaction by the Agency was swift. First, the CIA faced an immediate security concern. If more information emerged about the locations of facilities, those locations could face threats. Agency officers decided they had to move some prisoners, and they did so quickly. Meanwhile, the specificity in the articles suggested an insider leak. In November 2005, *Washington Post* journalist Dana Priest published an article under the headline, "CIA Holds Terror Suspects in Secret Prisons." The article covered the black site program and listed general locations of prison sites—"democracies in Eastern Europe"—but also two named countries.

The recognition of how quickly leaks could prompt the closure of a black site led to extensive planning about how to ensure rapid transfers. The pivot after that first major disclosure sparked a new way of thinking about the sites, and an assumption that each location would have a shelf life. Over time, CTC managers developed a three-tiered approach to detention facilities. The first-tier locations had prisoners. Other locations, a second tier, were empty but fully constructed, ready for occupation immediately if the populated sites needed to be closed in as little as a day or two. The third-tier prisons were under construction, not yet operational, ready to shift into operational status if the second-tier sites went live. This three-tier system became the standard for the black sites for a few years, with an expectation that each facility would have a lifespan of maybe a year. In the end, with the short duration of the Program, and the shift of prisoners to Guantanamo, some facilities were never occupied. It was another indicator of how quickly the CIA's detention operation grew and declined, in a matter of years.

Inside the Agency, the leaks from the disclosure of the Abu Zubaydah facility to the *Washington Post* in 2005 were viewed as severely damaging, not only because of the security risks they entailed but also because of the practical problem of shifting prisoners to new locations hosted by different allies. The hunt began immediately for the source of the leak. It was instantly clear that someone with access to details—accurate details—had provided the story to the *Post*. Knowledge of even the most secret CIA programs, though, wasn't limited to just a few people: field stations; headquarters managers; analysts; medical staff—the list of those who had some knowledge of the Program was large, and the investigation into the leak was extensive. Nonetheless, in a rare step, senior Agency managers ordered polygraphs for employees who knew about the Program. Agency officers are polygraphed regularly as part of standard security reinvestigations that also include financial checks and interviews with co-workers and friends. In this case, the polygraphs weren't general in nature.

Then, in the spring of 2006, the Agency announced that it had fired an employee in the CIA's Inspector General's office for unauthorized contact with the media, including the *Washington Post*. All Agency employees have signed secrecy agreements that preclude contact with the media outside authorized channels; the Agency contended that the employee had violated this agreement. Days after the announcement, the fired officer's lawyer acknowledged press contacts but denied that she was the source of the leaks about specific black site locations. With the acrimonious relationships between the IG and other Agency components already at a high state, the firing fed suspicions that the IG staff was riddled with personnel who had ethical qualms about the Program and used their positions to increase the pressure on the Agency to slow the Program and, ultimately, end it.

The public exposure led to difficult exchanges with allies about what was supposed to have been a highly secret enterprise. Former operations officers lament not the demise of the Program but the exposure of allies who were involved, and the violation of trust they felt after having assured partners of secrecy. That trust had grown in the early years of the counterterror campaign, when the CIA sent many of the detainee reports from Program prisoners to foreign security services. This is standard procedure for intelligence services: among friendly, or at least allied, services, sharing intelligence, even from sensitive sources, is routine. In the case of detainee reporting, the CIA masked the source of the reporting to obscure its origin, the same sort of masking the Agency did for intelligence consumers inside Washington. Hundreds of reports went out to foreign services between Abu Zubaydah's detention in 2002 and the news stories about secret black sites.

After the press revelations in 2005—particularly the news reports that European countries allowed CIA detention facilities on their soil—pressure started from foreign diplomats and politicians who had earlier asked few questions but now wanted specific details. These inquiries came from intelligence services that didn't host sites but received the intelligence "take," or reports, about detainees. The CIA didn't reveal what was going on with the Program, but some officers did make a critical point to their foreign partners: You know those hundreds of reports we sent you? Were those useful? Well, be careful. They are from the same Program you're asking us about. Overall, said one senior operations manager with decades of overseas experience, "They [one of the countries that hosted a black site] were more gracious than they should have been." This pattern of partnership that withstood the revelations, despite the tensions, held true with other countries as well.

At least two services asked, over time, for direct access to the detainees. They didn't know where they were held, or what the conditions were, but like any good intelligence service, they wanted to ask their own questions, unfiltered by the CIA—the same approach the CIA might take in a similar situation. The CIA declined, not out of a lack of trust but with the knowledge that if that service ever had a single officer visit a site, the service would be implicated in the Program. Touch a black site and you're radioactive, CIA officials reasoned. You may be frustrated because you know we're holding the biggest al-Qa'ida fish in the world. We are doing you a favor; sometime, down the line, you will thank us for not allowing you to get caught up in the inevitable attacks about detentions and interrogations. When your legislators ask what you knew, and when, you don't want to answer that you knew all along.

Now, lessons from inside government weren't the only drivers of the Program's evolution. Outside Langley, revelations about the country's aggressive counterterrorism operations had begun swirling. Even as early as 2005, just three years after the first black site opened, intelligence operations developed in the aftermath of 9/11 began to draw criticism, including from human rights groups, such as revelations that the National Security Agency had acquired massive amounts of data on Americans' phone calls to drone strikes against American citizens overseas and the future of prisoners at Guantanamo Bay.

Again, shifting legal positions marked a turning point for the Program, just as the hiatus in interrogations had in 2003. More

DoJ reconsiderations of the legal foundations came in May 2005, when different staff at the Office of Legal Counsel issued two additional memoranda. There was a strong working relationship between CIA lawyers and the Department of Justice, but some CIA executives were certain that, as with earlier covert action operations, the Program's participants too would be judged harshly, and other Washington agencies would try to sidestep responsibility. "Those people [at other Washington agencies] are going to fuck our people," one senior Program manager remembers thinking during some of the policy debates about the changing legal foundations. The Agency would not accept opinions that skirted the issue of the Program's legality; simply excusing the CIA from abiding by the US law and the Constitution itself, because the interrogations were conducted overseas, was never going to be an acceptable substitute for the first legal opinions.

By this time in 2005, the original DoJ drafters, particularly John Yoo and Jay Bybee, had left Justice. Their departures were critical: the legal foundations they established with their original memos were highly controversial, but they nonetheless issued what some DoJ observers later saw as not only aggressive but professionally questionable opinions. DoJ lawyers who had followed Yoo seemed skeptical that those first documents were solid, say CIA lawyers from that period. Yoo's successors weren't bent on closing down the Program, but they wanted to "get us into a space that was defensible," says one senior CIA lawyer. He continued: "I always felt DoJ was taking a reasonable and rational approach. If he [referring to one of Yoo's successors] had ever said, 'We can't support this,' Tenet and Goss would have suspended it." Nonetheless, the Department lawyers were looking. Again. Nobody blamed them, it was just another sign of the times.

These legal deliberations didn't happen in a vacuum. The

Inspector General had been reviewing the Program in 2004, and he presented his findings to the leadership of the Intelligence Committees in July. The echoes from the critiques of pre-9/11 operations were ringing through Washington then, adding emphasis to one of the responses to the IG's congressional presentation. One of the questioning responses, during an exchange that included the CIA General Counsel explaining that the Agency had suspended the Program pending further DoJ guidance, came from Senator Jay Rockefeller. The CIA, he countered, "needs to avoid risk aversion." Later, as details of the Program leaked to the media, members of Congress questioned whether the CIA had been forthcoming in its briefings of them. During the height of the Program, the message the CIA received was clear: America, through its elected representatives, is with us.

Again, the Agency looked to its own review to respond to the alarm bells about the legality and general appropriateness of the Program, so the Agency then looked to outsiders to conduct a bipartisan study conducted by non-CIA personnel. While it was such a touchy request and a number of candidates had already declined to participate, in the spring of 2005 Director Goss selected two well-known national security experts, Gardner Peckham and John Hamre, to conduct a review. However, in a nod to bipartisanship in Washington, Peckham was a prominent Republican; John Hamre had served as deputy secretary of Defense under President Clinton.

Goss's advisers gave Peckham and Hamre a simple mission: assess the effectiveness of the EITs and report back, in writing. They were given access to CIA messages, and they interviewed people who participated in and managed the Program. They were never told the locations of the black sites, but they did understand what happened after the moment of capture, from renditions through interrogations.

Tellingly, in political Washington, the two often worked separately, except for interviews of Agency officers that they conducted jointly. "I was deeply impressed," remembers one participant, reflecting on the management of the Program in the years after the early rough stages. The interviews also offered insights beyond whether the Program was administered properly. "I interviewed one psychologist," remembers this participant. "He was very upset, concerned about what was going to happen because of his participation." Like CIA staff overseeing the Program, the reviewers knew the long-term implications of their work. Said one,

> In my written report, I chose to judge the whole of the program, not just to assess the EITs, though I did that, too. I believe I assessed CTC compliance with DoJ guidelines, but in truth, I'm not a lawyer and of the assessments I did make, that may have been the least significant, but I felt it was important to do that. I knew at the time, that yesterday's actions would in the future be viewed through a different lens and the context would be lost, the context of the urgent need to better understand a mortal enemy that had us in his gun sights.

Part of the reason for the review was that Goss himself wanted answers about a controversial operation he was trying to grasp. As a former member of the congressional committee that oversaw CIA operations, he wanted to ensure that he had full visibility into any activities he hadn't seen in Congress. "We only knew what we were told," said one senior participant in that Congressional oversight process.

Clearly, with press revelations, DoJ shifts, and a generally souring mood in Washington about the CIA's interrogations, Agency officers inside Langley knew the unity of 2002 was long gone. In the midst of Goss's questions, the CIA faced another decision about how to protect Program participants under the assumption that this shifting mood eventually would result in attacks against the Agency, possibly including legal action. One long-debated area directly at the center involved, once again, Abu Zubaydah. Early in his interrogation, the Agency had made a fateful decision to videotape some interrogations. And the faces of some CIA officers were visible in those videos, along with the graphic brutality of the interrogations. Senior CIA officials had a problem on their hands. What if those tapes were to go public?

The initial decision to tape those interrogation sessions seems questionable in hindsight, but the thought process then underscores how CIA officers believed they were working with uniform political, and national, support, and how they anticipated that the support they felt would endure. The officers who remember the tapings also believed that if the Agency were criticized at some later date, the tapes would prove that the Agency interrogators applied interrogation techniques according to the policies and rules they were given.

Some officers saw the tapes as potential protection in the face of future criticism, diametrically opposite from the judgment that became obvious not long after. The tapes would raise a firestorm of criticism, and it wouldn't matter whether interrogators applied techniques according to the guidance they were given.[*] A picture is worth a thousand words, and the words to describe the techniques might seem dry in comparison to a full-action display of a shackled, hooded prisoner withstanding a harsh interrogation.

---

[*] The judgment about using tapes as a hedge against later accusations of prisoner abuse was not unique. Later, a program manager at another CIA black site, unaware of the swirl of controversy around the original tapes, asked whether his facility should begin taping interrogations. "No way," came the answer from CIA headquarters.

Some tapes showed waterboarding. Others sparked rare black humor. "At least they got the lawyers in the videos," a few CIA officers remarked.

The tapes stayed in a safe after their creation in 2002, not just to secure them but to ensure that they were unavailable to staff at the interrogation facilities. Shortly after they were created, a CIA manager at a black site witnessed visiting CIA security officers watching the videos. "For training purposes," the security officers said, in answer to a question about why they were viewing the tapes. "We want to be ready in case we are requested to assist." The staff at these facilities rotated in regularly; these were not long-term assignments. The manager's reaction was swift. "This wasn't Netflix," he remembers thinking. The tapes were moved to a safe at that facility until it closed, and they were then transported to the nearest CIA overseas office.

It soon became apparent that the tapes contained footage that was both brutal and threatened to expose the identities of interrogators who were at the facilities. In late 2005, Jose Rodriguez, then the CIA's DDO (Deputy Director for Operations, the powerful head of the Agency's overseas spy activities), made a decision that shadowed him for years. He ordered the destruction of the tapes, over the counsel of government lawyers, including the CIA's own general counsel. Many senior CIA officials, down through junior officers, applauded him. They viewed his order as an honorable step that reflected well on him personally. "He cared more about his people than he did for himself," says one former subordinate.

The Program managers in CTC, and CIA executives in seventh-floor leadership offices, did not and still do not view his action as a strictly legal or moral issue; instead, they almost uniformly believe he was responsible, as any head of operations would be, for protecting officers who were carrying out headquarters' orders that were legally authorized. Allowing the release of the tapes, in their view, would have jeopardized the officers who appeared on them. Most CIA officials from that era believe it was Rodriguez's responsibility to ensure that didn't happen. Further, they admire a step he took in light of the fact that it would almost certainly lead to censure, if not legal action. Later events proved them right, at least on the question of the risk he took in issuing the order. He was investigated by a federal prosecutor for years about that decision, though the case was closed in 2010.

Rodriguez's lightning-rod decision to destroy the tapes is generally respected among CIA officers many years later. Part of this perspective reflects Agency culture. Compared to other Washington-area bureaucracies, particularly the Pentagon, the CIA is a relatively small organization, and its officers pride themselves on their agility, elite cadre, and ability to operate effectively in a wide variety of difficult foreign environments, from Moscow to Afghanistan. The organization is tight-knit enough that senior officers know each other well, and they are accustomed to operating together, especially overseas, in situations where they are cleared to make their own rules, and where they protect their own. Rodriguez wanted to move to protect Agency officers.

CIA members also point to Rodriguez's personality when they assess the decision. He had built a reputation as an action-oriented officer who was less concerned with the niceties of bureaucracies or language than he was with action, any action. Errors of commission—doing things—were always better than errors of omission, which were anathema in the post-9/11 CIA world of high risk, high reward. He was not viewed as rash; he was seen as likely to take risks, even if the consequences were negative, and as accepting risk with a shrug of the shoulders. His action-oriented personality, coupled with the Agency's culture of making the rules fit the circumstances, led to the decision that embroiled him in legal wrangling after he ordered the tapes' destruction.

Rodriguez remembers thinking about the decision for months and then years. "Somebody has to make a decision," he remembers thinking. The Abu Ghraib scandal played into the Washington paralysis; how could a senior official decide to authorize destruction of the tapes in the wake of the Iraq prison scandal? Finally, Rodriguez recalls returning to the decision while cutting the grass at his home one weekend. "Nobody will make this decision. So I will." It wasn't a rash choice, or a reflection of petulance. Rodriguez thought he had to act.

The challenges mounted. As General Michael Hayden took office as CIA director in May 2006, he found a Program that was not sustainable. Was the DoJ position untenable, as lawyers who were not involved in the original guidance questioned their predecessors? Were the techniques effective? Should the CIA be in the interrogation business at all? And, of course, the final question: What was going to happen to these detainees? Early on, senior CIA officials repeated to him what the Agency had been saying internally and at secret Washington meetings for years. One former senior CIA official remembers the message as being simple: "We aren't jailers, we need a solution."

Most immediately, though, Hayden dealt with yet another legal hurdle. The Program faced another suspension at the time of Hayden's arrival at the Agency, stemming from a Supreme Court decision (*Hamdan v. Rumsfeld*, decided by the Court in 2006) about the government's potential prosecution of terrorists through military commissions. The decision extended Article 3 of the Geneva Convention—including language about the treatment of prisoners, such as a provision against "humiliating and degrading treatment"—to al-Qa'ida. The Agency once again turned to the White House and DoJ for another paper. Their view was simple: we can't move again without documentation. They got it in 2007, with President Bush and the Department of Justice issuing guidance on the remaining CIA techniques. One last time, the Program was back in business.

One executive-suite staff officer, referring to CIA director Hayden, commented on his motivation to ensure that every move included specific legal guidance. "He [Hayden] was emotional about wanting to establish a program that would protect the people in the program." Everyone knew that the sands in Washington had shifted to defense, ensuring that those who had been involved would be shielded from blowback.

Hayden also had his own questions about the Program. Shortly after he became director, he ordered a full-scale review of detainee practices that many officers still remember. Like other senior security officials in Washington, Hayden was broadly aware that the Program existed. Details about it were not generally discussed, even with his experience as the director of the National Security Agency prior to becoming CIA director. So Hayden went into the Agency with hard questions about the effectiveness of the Program and its implementation. He also knew that unease about the Program was growing in Washington. He wanted to learn for himself, partly to prepare for the inevitable heat that would surround the Program whenever it was revealed.

Hayden had not only the pedigree to ask good questions, he had the leadership skills to win over the workforce and the toughness to push ahead when he found resistance. He wasn't a screamer—on the contrary, he came across as serious and studied, and his immersion in the details of the Program left some on the seventh floor with the sense that he knew more than the staff. He was smart and dogged, and he pressed for details on the Program so he could find his own answers rather than depending solely on officers whose history in the Program might lead them to mask its secrets.

In retrospect, through Hayden's tenure as CIA director (2006–2009), it was clear that the story of one of the most aggressive, unique, and hotly debated operations in CIA history was drawing to a close: there was the internal scrutiny at Langley, the growing media exposure on the outside, the IG pressure, the questioning at DoJ. There was still one insoluble problem, though, that wasn't close to resolution: what to do with the prisoners when they no longer had intelligence value. How to find a permanent home for them when the government-wide support for an almost "anything goes" approach was fraying, alongside popular sentiment. It was the one question that remained, and nobody in decision-making positions wanted to come up with answers.

14

Endgame

From the director on down, every senior CIA official involved in the Program knew that the Agency couldn't hold prisoners forever. As one senior official later reflected, "This wasn't what we did."

The Agency already had years of experience with one potential long-term solution: Guantanamo Bay, where the first prisoners of the terror war arrived in early 2002 from the Afghan battlefield and beyond. Shortly after the decision to create a detention facility at Guantanamo, officers from the Counterterrorism Center visited the prison to plot out how to question the detainees who were transferred there. It was clear that this mass influx of captives—not the high-end al-Qa'ida detainees who went to the secret black sites but lower-level Taliban and al-Qa'ida prisoners, who might have snippets of intelligence—would be worth talking to. This was a serious undertaking: not only did the Agency have to create the interrogation rooms themselves for these second- and third-tier detainees, they also had to house personnel and plan for the steady stream of foreign intelligence services who would want to visit so that they could question the prisoners from their countries.

Guantanamo wasn't an option until later in the Bush Administration because of the still-secret interrogation practices the Agency was using at black sites. Prisoners at Guantanamo had access to the Red Cross, and the location was too open for a covert operation to remain shrouded. Journalists and foreign security services often visited. That said, it was not an option for Program prisoners who had already gone through intensive interrogations.

The conversations about what to do long-term had started as early as 2003, but they didn't gain traction. In that year, one of the Program managers remembers Agency leaders already reaching the conclusion that they had to find a stable location for years of detention. The options were captured in what Tenet referred to as one of his periodic "deep dives," an in-depth discussion about any issue of importance. In this case, the senior briefer arrived with about ten PowerPoint slides, listing options ranging from releasing prisoners to holding them forever. On the last page was the term that would haunt Agency leaders for years: "Endgame," the shorthand for the final disposition for the prisoners. And that's what it was called, for years after.

The Inspector General report from 2004 offered a flavor of those early endgame considerations and the underlying frustrations of the CIA as it grappled with long-term detainees and Washington's unwillingness to come up with solutions: "Although there has been ongoing discussion of the [endgame] issue inside the agency and among NSC [White House National Security Council], Defense Department, and Justice Depart-

ment officials, no decisions on any 'endgame' for Agency detainees have been made. Senior Agency officials see this as a policy
issue for the U.S. Government rather than a CIA issue. Even
with Agency initiatives to address endgame with policymakers,
some detainees who cannot be prosecuted will likely remain in
CIA custody indefinitely."

Endgame had gained some momentum under Porter Goss,
who became CIA director in 2004, but it didn't start to reach
closure until it became clear that President Bush didn't want to
leave the issue to his successor. The value of the detainees was
inarguably declining, to the point where some who had been
held for long periods could provide very little. The priority for
them shifted to ensuring that they stayed occupied. Others were
lower-ranking; they simply didn't have enough depth of knowledge about al-Qa'ida to be useful intelligence sources after they
gave up the basics of what they knew. By 2007, when Bush was
thinking about his handoff to a new president and the endgame
process neared its conclusion, some at the Agency referred to
these prisoners as "empties"—prisoners whose lives as valuable sources of intelligence were spent and who became, in CIA
facilities, everyday detainees. One of the CIA officials involved
in negotiating the endgame process remembers his sentiments:
"We had to get rid of them. They're scattered [across different
black sites]. The host countries are not happy."

They were also a growing risk. If one were to die at a detention facility, the Agency would face questions in which no
answer would be good enough. In addition, time didn't favor
the Agency: with sometimes skittish partners overseas, and the
growing media attention, more detainees meant a greater black
site footprint, which in turn meant a greater chance of exposure.

The detainees were psychological hazards as much as they

were physical risks. Some were in detention so long that it was difficult to find diversions to occupy their time. Long after these detainees had become compliant, they shared down-time with their interrogators. Watching videos. Playing games. Talking, sometimes for long hours, about the history of jihad and al-Qa'ida. They read books. Khalid Shaykh Mohammed had an engineering bent. He requested, and received, designs for vacuum cleaners. He said he wanted to come up with bet-ter designs.

The top-to-bottom review Hayden ordered in 2006 led him to conclude that the Agency had to slim down the Program to make it sustainable. Hayden became convinced that the intelli-gence acquired in the Program was valuable, alongside the huge volumes of email, phone, and human source data the Agency was vacuuming up. To try to ensure sustainability, waterboard-ing was dropped, since it had been used against so few detain-ees. Overall, the number of approved techniques after the review slipped to six, about half the number of techniques approved at the Program's outset. Said one of Hayden's advisers, "We had to make this America's Program."

One reason the narrower guidelines met with no opposition was that the Agency officers felt, by the time they faced questions from Hayden, that they had a much greater understanding of the dynamics of interrogations. They knew what worked—sleep deprivation, for example, and walling—and they knew how to build individual interrogation modules in ways they could not have understood in the early days. Some interrogators thought they had become so knowledgeable about, and proficient in, the application of techniques that they could focus on just a few and still achieve results consistently. Some interrogators thought they had learned so much about the effectiveness of less brutal techniques that waterboarding wouldn't be necessary. CIA officers universally saw it as unquestionably effective; for many, though, it was just too controversial.

Still, the endgame loomed. Even the high-level meetings at the White House offered a clue about how secret, and controversial, the endgame conversation remained in Hayden's tenure. Meetings at the White House just below the Cabinet level often are referred to as "DCs," or Deputies' Committees, the meetings of the second-ranking officials at major government departments. The informal name for the endgame meetings? "Un-DCs," remembers an Agency observer.

Agency officials saw an endgame process that was stuck in neutral, and they were growing frustrated, sensing that they had been left holding the bag. Washington had supported the Agency when times were tough, with the universally accepted fight against al-Qa'ida in 2001 and after. Now, as the national mood shifted, those CIA officials thought the same senior executives in government who had supported the Program shied away from a decision that proved far tougher than authorizing the interrogations in the first place. The White House initially had provided the presidential backing to initiate and continue the Program because of the unity of purpose in government then and the commonly held view that the prisoners' knowledge outweighed the risks of the Program. Even two years after the Agency had the prisoners, nobody wanted to discuss the consequences, particularly the public reckoning that would have to happen if the prisoners were transferred out of CIA custody and into a public facility. Everyone knew the questioning and criticism that would ensue once the Program went overt.

The frustrations at Langley translated into tense policy meetings under Goss and Hayden, partly because CIA officials wanted closure. The two sides—senior administration officials, including White House personnel, on one side and the CIA seventh-floor executives on the other—were entrenched in their views. The policy debate was a stalemate: the White House and others saw no place to transfer the prisoners. They didn't want to add more detainees to the Guantanamo base. The Agency was similarly stubborn. The prisoners have to go sooner or later, Langley argued again and again, and we have to get out of the jail business. The mistrust between the Pentagon and the Agency on detainee issues festered. In 2006 and beyond, after the Abu Ghraib scandal had begun to recede, one seventh-floor executive summed up the Agency's view of the Pentagon in simple terms, "DoD is going Greenpeace on us."

Agency officers from that Goss-Hayden endgame era remember one standoff clearly. A senior executive remembers there being about a half-dozen other senior officials gathered to converse with the Bush White House. Near the end of the negotiations, the Agency issued a warning that, according to the participant, broke the logjam. "Either put them in Gitmo [Guantanamo Bay]," he remembers saying, "or we are sending them back to their countries of origin."

Bush was ready to move. Despite the Ghraib mess and questions about the long-term disposition of Guantanamo Bay prisoners, transfer there seemed the only option. The president told an interagency meeting of senior officials that he would make the announcement, closing what had been a long, meandering debate about endgame for the CIA's black sites and enhanced interrogation techniques. The CIA officers who were preparing for the closure of the Program knew the next step: after the president brought into the open what many had known for years, the Program would close and the CIA would have to answer for those years of black sites and harsh interrogations.

The president knew that the public questions would be tough. On his way out of that meeting in 2006 he turned to a CIA official who was attending. "Make sure you check my speech, every detail. And then check it again." Every word would be picked over. And during the ensuing decade, every move the CIA had made in designing and implementing the Program would be examined again.

The door wasn't fully closing, though. Says one lawyer involved in that stage, "Part of what we had to do was look at whether drafts of the speech would have the president saying so much that we would be unable to continue in the future. He could admit the past. We spent weeks with [presidential speechwriter] Marc Thiessen." They were ensuring that the final draft of the speech would meet the president's intent that the Agency maintain the option of accepting more prisoners.

As the president prepared to announce the existence of the Program to the American people in mid-2006, a final group of more than a dozen detainees had to be moved. There wasn't much time, and the logistics weren't perfect. Because of the political sensitivities of touching down on foreign soil with that group on a large US government transport aircraft, the Agency planned the transfer with multiple in-flight refuelings to keep the aircraft flying.

Hayden wanted to ensure it all went off without a hitch. On the evening the detainees were making the trip, he was at a social engagement without access to a secure telephone. So he and the manager of the flight transfer arranged a uniquely American signal. "I've got to know when the plane is wheels up," one manager recalls him saying. "Whenever that happens, you call me. And

you tell me that Elvis has left the theater." Hayden got the call.
The flight went off without problems.

The morning after the transfer, Director Hayden was handed
a scorecard. He, like many managers at the Agency, was keeping track of how many detainees the CIA still had. On the front
of the scorecard was the reckoning of who the Agency had held
during those final days. On the back of the card was the updated
number. Zero.

President Bush announced the final transfer of CIA detainees to Guantanamo Bay in September 2006, in a televised statement. He also ignited a debate that continues among former (and
current) CIA officers. In the speech, he defended the detention
and interrogation of al-Qa'ida members and took a step further:
he declined to rule out reinstating the Program at a later date.
"The current transfers mean that there are now no terrorists in
the CIA program," Bush announced. "But as more high-ranking
terrorists are captured, the need to obtain intelligence from them
will remain critical, and having a CIA program for questioning terrorists will continue to be crucial to getting lifesaving
information."

The Program was in its death throes. But it wasn't dead yet,
even with the fact that there weren't any prisoners left. The CIA
would send just a few more detainees to black sites into 2007,
but the Agency was far more cautious about which prisoners to
send there after the public announcement. Standards were high:
senior CIA executives didn't want to take new prisoners unless
the potential upside, the intelligence value of the prisoners, was
beyond any dispute. And the use of enhanced techniques, the
half-dozen that were still authorized under Hayden, came under
far more senior review.

Hayden and officials around him, some relatively new to the

detention and interrogation business, were convinced that the Program was still producing positive results, and they were ready to continue to authorize tough measures. The entire foundation of interrogations, though, had flipped. CIA executives universally speak about one of their basic motivations as the Program was set up in 2002: What happens if we don't do this? In 2005–6, the question was entirely different: What happens if we continue this? What are the risks? These questions became urgent, and primary, when the Abu Ghraib scandal broke. One long-time Agency executive spoke of the change in tone as reflecting, in part, how far the country had come. "In 2006," he says, "five years after the attacks, it might as well have been 500."

Even within the CIA, though, the seventh-floor executive staff sensed interrogation fatigue. Said one official from the Agency's executive wing then, "We were in a different place. We actually knew a lot [about al-Qa'ida]," echoing a view that many counterterrorism specialists and managers shared, then and now. He went on. "So we need to devise a program that gets us info in a sustainable fashion, knowing that we now have a lot of knowledge. It was maybe a more seasoned, rational, reflective time. We have to make this America's program." Part of that process involved another round of briefings on Capitol Hill in late 2006, presenting the new, trimmed Program.

Into 2007, Hayden and his team continued to engage congressional overseers as he adjusted the Program. They spoke with both the Senate and House oversight committees—including John McCain, who wasn't formally part of the oversight committee but was seen as a critical player on the interrogation issue because of his POW history—about the revised Program parameters. CIA officials remember the Congress as being supportive; they didn't get ringing endorsements, but neither did they hear opposition from the committees. McCain was another story; he was vociferous in his critiques, temperamental and explosive during some exchanges with the Agency, say some CIA officials.

Program oversight reached the point, near the end in 2007, where staff assistants in the Agency's seventh-floor executive wing were calculating the hours of sleep deprivation individual prisoners were enduring while their interrogations were ongoing. The CIA executive suite, in other words, was interpreting the guidance from the Department of Justice to ensure that the Agency was complying with the precise letter of the direction they had received. They compared notes with the Agency element that managed the operations, to ensure everybody had a common understanding of how they were interpreting their guidance. Sometimes the two Agency elements differed. If a detainee was allowed a certain amount of sleep during a two-week period, for example, how should you measure that period? Would it be one defined fourteen-day block—say, the first through the fourteenth of the month? Or would the period proceed on a rolling scale, with the clock never resetting? From a Program that had started without clear guidelines at Catseye, within the space of a few years different headquarters elements were comparing notes on how much sleep individual prisoners were allowed.

More decisions went upstairs to the executive suite, and Hayden was personally involved in authorizing transfers to black sites. After the Bush speech, one of the transfers was a senior figure in al-Qa'ida circles who chose to talk without undergoing harsh interrogations. He was an example of why the interrogators had set up their interactions with detainees to begin with a neutral probe. Later in 2007 the CIA sent one more detainee to a black site. This time, the response was different: he refused to speak. One final time, the interrogation team used the tough interrogation tools to see if he would answer questions, to see if, once more, they could press a prisoner into compliance.

It didn't work.* Sleep deprivation was one of the key techniques used with him, and the level of scrutiny reached the point where CIA director Hayden signed off on the final effort to subject the detainee to one more round of sleep deprivation. He resisted.

Now, in 2007, it was as if everybody was watching. Through that final period, Hayden and Washington politicians and policymakers weren't operating in a vacuum. The Program had mushroomed from an occasional story in major newspapers to a prominent national security lightning rod that drew regular coverage. The *New York Times*, for example, published articles through 2007 detailing debates about detainee policy within the Bush administration. The dates and headlines of some of those stories offer a picture of how far media coverage had progressed in the five short years since Abu Zubaydah's capture.

May 2007: Interrogation Methods Are Criticized
June 2007: Soviet Style 'Torture' Becomes 'Interrogation'
October 2007: Secret U.S. Endorsement of Severe
    Interrogations
November 2007: A Firsthand Experience before Decision
    on Torture

---

* One senior manager from that time recalls adding a Post-it note to a document sent to Hayden from within the CIA about this final sleep-deprivation attempt. "I don't want to write this formally," the manager remembers saying, "but I should tell you this won't work." Somewhere along the chain, as the memo was transmitted upstairs to Director Hayden's office, the note apparently fell off or was removed by a staff officer.

In the spy world, "covert action" by definition is supposed to remain secret. Clearly, by 2007, the secret was out, but the Program was already dying. The door on the Program shut forever with the election of President Obama. Initially, some senior CIA officials thought they could explain the interrogation process to the president; it wasn't clear whether he already had iron-clad views on harsh interrogations. The idea was for a few officials, including Director Hayden, to travel to President-elect Obama's offices in Chicago to explain the Program and also to get hands-on, demonstrating some of the interrogation techniques in the Chicago office.

A small team took a trip, visiting not only Obama but a few of his advisers, after the election, before the inauguration. One senior CIA executive demonstrated a facial slap on one attendee at a briefing on the Program. CIA officers have different recollections of that briefing. Some walked away thinking it was effective. Another senior CIA official offers a different perspective. "The reaction was negative," he says. The effort to slim down the Program to ensure it would endure didn't last.

The new president spoke publicly about the Program soon after he took office. His views were clear in closed discussions among staff at the White House, but they burst into the open more bluntly during a press conference in August 2014, years after the Program had been shuttered. Using words that still echo across the CIA, the president said some officials had "crossed a line." He added, "We did a whole lot of things that were right, but we tortured some folks," remarks made in response to the impending release of a major Senate report on the Program. If there was any doubt about many CIA officials' early predictions about the boomerang effect of Agency covert actions—that succeeding generations would look back in history and judge Agency officials harshly—those doubts were gone. The president continued,

"We did some things that were contrary to our values." What was once backed by a president, authorized by the Department of Justice, and briefed to the Congress, was now seen as a violation of the country's profoundly held view that the United States held the moral high ground. One president authorized the Program; within a few years, the next had attacked it.

15

Ethics and Reflections

The CIA officers who led, designed, managed, participated in, and observed the Program are unapologetic today about what they did. They believe that the range of steps the Agency took, including the detention and interrogation program, prevented what seemed inevitable in September 2001: a Second Wave. Those officials now reflect on those years with a near-unanimous view that they participated in a unique operation that helped stem the tide of al-Qa'ida, and that their successes allowed for the debates about the Program that followed. Had al-Qa'ida conducted further catastrophic attacks, they say, there wouldn't be a debate about interrogations. The debate instead would focus on why the Agency hadn't done more.

Many will never speak publicly about their participation or their views. For some, their oaths of secrecy still hold, even after years of public revelations about a Program they were once sworn to protect and that presidents have now acknowledged. For others, the experiences in the years after the Program's exposure have led them to let the history and the memories fade. They know what they did, and why, and they see little reason to return to defend what was once, in their eyes, a Program that reflected the policy, law, and national will of America. Their sense of accomplishment is tempered by frustration, though, sometimes mixed with anger, that some of the same political players who gave them assurances during the early years later painted them as rogue operators.

The working-level architects of the Program and long-time senior executives who served at its inception had few illusions about how they might be judged when the Program and its details came to light. Generations of CIA officers have relived, over decades, after-the-fact judgments about controversial covert actions that once were deemed legal and appropriate and later seen as rogue or well beyond the pale of acceptable. Today's political leaders might not support a controversial covert action, they know, because they see a threat that later leaders will view as less compelling. Succeeding generations grapple with the rationale for these operations. It's a cycle that has dogged the Agency since its inception. Clandestine operations are the dark side of diplomacy, the activities political leaders authorize when they do not want American fingerprints on a controversial policy. Presidents don't authorize secret operations because they're pretty. They're deniable—designed for the US government to operate behind a cloak of secrecy when conducting operations that nobody wants to acknowledge.

The national mood, reflected through elected officials, was critical in affecting their judgment about proceeding with the Program. Several take a step further, saying they believe the shutdown of the Program after a relatively short period of time was the right step. In their view, by 2007 the time had come; even then, a half-decade after the attacks, the country's mood had changed dramatically—as had the mood in Congress—and the Agency's progress against al-Qa'ida had already been marked.

Many of them ask now what options would have been more palatable, particularly given the tenor of the times. And they reject the notion that there were easy answers. Some now separate waterboarding from the remainder of the techniques as an especially tough tactic. Most would not revisit their decision to support, or manage, the interrogation program; they would reconsider using waterboarding as a technique. They question whether the views of the Program would differ if the lightning-rod issue of waterboarding were off the table, if the Agency had only used other tactics. On this issue, too, their views are consistent: if it wasn't waterboarding, it would be some other tactic. The criticism was inevitable, in their eyes. Says one longtime CTC officer who helped oversee the Program, "Waterboarding is the most visual of them all."

In retrospect, many officers see waterboarding as an easy target for critics, a source of debate that draws attention away from subtler, more meaningful conversations about the appropriateness of harsh interrogations in a democratic society. They often point to the fact that only three of more than a hundred CIA detainees were waterboarded, and they see the focus on those three detainees as diverting from more difficult questions: What about sleep deprivation, for example? If the public debate centered on that tactic, would the conversation end up in a different place? Sleep deprivation doesn't involve physical contact with the detainee; does that change critics' views? Is any pressure on a detainee acceptable?

Some Agency officers, though not a majority, also reflect on inflection points that they believe could have resulted in a more thorough review of whether and how to continue the Program at some intermediate stage, even if they doubt that substantial change would have resulted. "At the beginning, you're operating at that visceral survival level," said one CIA official of the early period. Over time, as the threat of an imminent attack slowly faded and the Agency's understanding of al-Qa'ida improved, some believe there should have been a more purposeful examination of whether the Program outlived its usefulness. Even those who have questions about the appropriateness of the Program acknowledge that the motivations in those early, tense months were understandable. They are less certain that those same motivations should have driven the continuation of the Program as the years passed.

One of the most senior officials from the latter stages of the Program points to a key decision, from Abu Zubaydah's interrogation through the final stages of the Program: he, and others, remember thinking more about how long to authorize the continuation of techniques, particularly sleep deprivation, than about whether to initiate harsh interrogations. His hesitation highlights one of the challenges in evaluating each individual prisoner, what that prisoner might reveal, and when that prisoner reaches an end point, unwilling to reveal more. In one case, this senior manager says he regrets authorizing the continuation of a sleep deprivation regimen. The prisoner had said all he was going to say. The additional time proved unproductive.

Few believe there would have been much opposition to continuing the Program had there been a more formal process to review the decisions of the early post-attack period. Inside the management hierarchy of the Program, from directors on down, senior officers and mid-level managers do not remember internal criticisms of the Program from any front, except the Inspector General. Staff officers, whether they believed in the interrogation methods or felt overwhelmed by the bureaucratic drive of their colleagues—and the pervasive sense that the Agency was ordered by the president and others to do whatever it took to stop al-Qa'ida—supported the Program. In retrospect, some officers who came later do not see the Program in an entirely positive light, but they believe its benefits outweighed the costs. One former senior official who participated in the endgame negotiations with the White House reflects on what he saw on the inside at the Agency and how he now balances the pluses and minuses. "Neutral plus," he now says.

Though officials from that era do not remember much internal opposition, some do recall conversations with employees outside the Program who said they opposed the techniques as unethical. Some differed. "I belonged to a frat house," says one, "and what we did to pledges was worse than this." There seemed to be an inverse relationship between the likelihood an officer would question the Program and the distance that officer sat from the Counterterrorism Center. The rise of drone warfare led some CIA officials who were worried about the inevitable tide turning against the Agency to compare targeted drone killings with the interrogations.

The management lapses, particularly the lax oversight in the pre-Program Salt Pit era, evoke a different response. Many CIA officials, from senior ranks down, reflect on those early days of CIA detentions, and readily accept that they were too lax in providing oversight, and not aggressive enough in understanding just how risky and complex detainee management proved to be.

Personal soul searching came both on the spot and over time. Some reflected deeply on the path they were on; others quickly came to their own personal understandings of the appropriateness of what they were doing. In addition to forcing CIA officials to confront the question of where to house this new type of prisoner, Abu Zubaydah's capture left all Agency officers asking how to weigh the ethics of what they had never been trained to contemplate, much less manage. These ethical questions played out in private; meetings and internal deliberations at the Agency typically centered on questions of law, policy, congressional notification, procedures for the sites—the kind of internal and intra-Washington coordination that the Agency does on sensitive covert programs. This program, though, was viewed as hypersensitive, and more radioactive, than more traditional operations the Agency had long undertaken, such as secretly aiding foreign rebels or using psychological operations to undermine foreign governments.

Some reflected on their own, and some talked to colleagues outside the normal meeting regimen. One operations manager from the early days of the Program recalls long after-hours conversations with a colleague who was one of the architects of the Program. Senior officers from that time say the ethics issues—from the big question of whether America should be in the harsh interrogation business to more granular questions about Geneva Convention requirements—were prominent as they hashed out, for themselves, how they could accept the path the Agency took. Most officers from that era did not discuss their views of the ethics of harsh interrogations in formal groups, but they all say that they thought about the morality of the Program, then and now.

One senior manager from that era, involved in the evaluations of Abu Zubaydah, summarized the ethical issues in five key questions based on his long reflections about the ethics of the Program after he retired from the CIA. He cites Rushworth Kidder, a leading expert in the application of ethics to decision-making, as a source who later helped him break down the way he came to think about those choices more than a decade ago.[*] His summary was captured in five quick tests about tough right-and-wrong decisions that help clarify the interrogation thinking:

- Is it legal?
- Is it the local version of legal (in other words, does it comply with company/agency/group)?
- Would you be ashamed to have it played out on the front page of the newspaper? Just the facts, not spun by an editorial page, and with a few paragraphs on your motivations? (The *Washington Post* test, in other words.)
- Would your mom (or any individual you see as a strong moral guide) be ashamed if she knew all?
- Does it pass a simple smell test; do you sense that it is wrong?

The first two are red flags, he says. If you're violating them, whatever action you're considering is inappropriate. The final three are yellow flags: you can violate them, but not without thinking long and hard.

He says, today, that he believes the CIA passed all five, though not with flying colors.

- The Attorney General told us it was legal, and gave us a written opinion. Lawmakers didn't question the legality.
- The CIA didn't have regulations or policy on this when its officers developed the program. They made policy on the fly. When they violated their own policies, they disci-

---

[*] Kidder studied practical solutions for ethical problems and authored *How Good People Make Tough Choices: Resolving the Dilemmas of Ethical Living.*

plined officers, and referred a few to the Department of Justice for potential prosecution.

- The newspaper test is dicier. In 2002, he says, America would have said, in short, "fine." A decade later, when Americans were asked about what they read in a widely publicized, and harsh, Senate review of the Program, polling still showed most Americans accepted what the Agency had done, despite the massive change in national concern about terrorism, and the lack of catastrophic attacks after 9/11.

- The mom test, this official says, is mixed. "My mother," he reflects, "would have said, 'I raised you better, don't do this.' My father would have said this is war, and I fought a war. This is what happens in war."

- The smell test. "Yeah, it stunk," he says. "So did not getting the intelligence that al-Qa'ida was plotting the 9/11 attacks."

Weighing these five judgments together, this officer captures what many officers struggle to explain. "This was an ugly thing to be involved in. The question, though, is different: Can I live with it? Do I walk away? I wrestled with the ethics of coercing another human being," he says, "even when I knew it was legally blessed. When you're in new ethical territory, you have to draw lines carefully so that momentum doesn't take you across a line without thinking." Like many officers, the fact that US military personnel had endured similar tactics in SERE school gave him a rough baseline: the CIA, he thought, shouldn't do anything to which it won't subject its own officers. "That's how I racked it up at the time," he explains, "and how formal training came together to help me characterize my thinking later. We came out in the right place. And I feel comfortable that I would come out in the same place again if we were to do it again."

In the end, after answering these questions for himself, he came up with a one-sentence summary that captures the grim acceptance of the Program that characterizes many officers' views: "It doesn't mean that it's the right thing to do, it means that it's not the wrong thing to do." Another was more prosaic. "You just suck it up," he says; "life sucks, it will suck more, I just hope they don't prosecute me. People say, 'Well, yeah, isn't that what the CIA does?'"

Behind the sense of accomplishment about blocking another catastrophic attack, and the frustrations of the later recriminations, Agency officers continued to think about the personal cost of what they witnessed or oversaw. It was never an easy operation for participants, even as it was underway. They dismiss Hollywood characterizations of CIA officers relishing the chance to rough up detainees—"There were no big threats [at the black sites], no hollering," remembers one CIA interrogator—and they see these movie and TV dramas as feeding a popular perception that the Agency somehow operates in a gray zone, outside the law and ethical boundaries. Looking back, says one operations officer who reviewed the Program, "There is a national amnesia by people who weren't involved who want to make themselves feel better. At the time, I guarantee that 99 percent of them would have said ok."

Those questions about judgments made years later, after the national hysteria surrounding 9/11 had slowly subsided, were confirmed by the government's own treatment of key architects of the Program. The initial drafters of the DoJ opinions, John Yoo and Jay Bybee, faced blunt censure in a July 2009 judgment that assessed they had engaged in "professional misconduct." A subsequent DoJ review rejected that charge but still faulted the legal analysis. "While I have declined to adopt O.P.R.'s [DoJ's Office of Professional Responsibility] findings of misconduct," wrote the senior reviewing official at DoJ, "I fear that John Yoo's loyalty to his own ideology and convictions clouded his view of his obligation to his client and led him to author opinions that reflected his own extreme, albeit sincerely held, view of executive power while speaking for an institutional client." In 2007, Yoo and Bybee's main partner at the CIA, John Rizzo, was nominated to be the Agency's top lawyer. His involvement in the detention and interrogation also sealed his fate: his nomination was blocked because of it.

As CIA officers discuss these issues, often more than a decade after they left the Agency, emotions run high, particularly on the use of shorthand today to describe the complex interrogation tactics: "torture."

CIA officers talk about how they had to come face-to-face with a simple question: what qualifies as torture, and are these tactics even close? They bristle at what they see as the simplicity of the debate among critics; beyond the universal judgment that torture is wrong and a constitutional violation in all circumstances, they do not believe the public debate forces everyday observers to amplify what they mean by torture. For example, under the definition of an incarceration measure that will result in long-term psychological damage, some point to solitary confinement as far more severe than any tactic the CIA ever employed, because prisoners in solitary suffer mental problems that result directly from their lack of contact with other humans.

Beyond the legal and political justifications CIA officers give, many point to a more basic and nuanced defense of their actions. They do not believe what they engaged in was torture measured by the standards from the Department of Justice or the broader moral terms they use as benchmarks for the techniques the Agency developed. Rather than the loaded term "torture," they see the debate crystallizing around clearer points. Is sleep deprivation wrong, in the environment that they were operating in during the early 2000s? Over what period of time? Does your scale change depending on the country's mood, or who the detainee is?

Stepping back to the uncertainty and immediacy of the time, though, officers who were there would ask more difficult questions. Was what we did never justified? And if not, why was there such a broad, universal acceptance of and support for the Program, by the executive and legislative branches? Why did an entire tier of Americans support what we did then, yet as the attacks have slipped slowly into history, decide that the standard we used then is somehow wrong?

Agency officials reflect on these judgments about the past—how American attitudes changed, how some CIA activities were supported by one president and vilified by the next—to look to the future, particularly the question of what America might do if faced with another 9/11-type tragedy. There are differences of opinion about how future Agency officers would respond to a presidential order to create a new detention and interrogation program. Their responses are marked by subtleties, but many do not rule out the possibility, even with the judgment that any controversial covert action program, including an altered detention program, would lead to more harsh criticism, or even legal action. One of the more equivocal senior officers still doesn't know, and his judgment reflects the concern that another attack will raise the same questions about the role of the CIA. "I felt ambivalent about the entire Program," he says, "but I wouldn't say we shouldn't do it again."

Some of the officers who participated offer an unequivocal "yes," typically those officers who were most strident during the time the Program was active. Others answer in the negative, not because they see the Program as wrong but because they have witnessed the consequences, what they regard as the attacks on Agency officers who were conducting a legally and politically authorized covert action. These officers, often former senior managers, say they would not subject subordinates to the risk of running another program if they were in management positions today and a catastrophic attack led another president to reconsider the use of the black sites.

Many point to a distinction between how senior ranks, particularly future directors, and junior ranks might respond. The Agency rank-and-file are not shy about offering critiques to senior managers, but they do believe they have a responsibility to respond to elected officials in times of crisis, and to the American people. And they do understand that they operate in a secret world that is by its very nature controversial. Though there are mixed views on whether a future CIA director would accept a presidential order to reopen the Program, former CIA officials are more uniform in their view that subordinates would follow the lead of a director who accepted the order. "Agency officers do what they're told," says one of the managers who oversaw the Agency as the Program waned. Even those who would support the institution of another Program, if they saw the nation at risk, would not include waterboarding among the list of tactics they would employ. They know the later repercussions would echo what they have witnessed over the past decade.

It's not clear that American policymakers will ever again use the interrogation program that the CIA developed. Participants say it won't matter: since a core element of the Program was the unknown, to ensure that detainees did not know what their futures held and how long they could withstand the techniques, a future generation couldn't rely on the same tactics. Public revelations about the Program—and its limitations, particularly the relatively limited timeframe during which techniques were applied against individual prisoners and the practice of never ensuring long-term psychological or physical damage—mean that future adversaries can practice how to counter the techniques.

Some senior officials talk about memories of feeling that they had little choice but to start, or continue, the Program. One recollects hearing a few details about the Program before his arrival at the CIA from another intelligence agency. "I'm glad I don't have to make those decisions," he remembers thinking. Nevertheless, after his arrival at CIA, he found himself in the same decision-making seat. His recollection is clear, and it is the same sort of mentality many officers say they had in the first half-dozen years after 9/11. "I really don't want to do this," he remembers. He also recalls the overwhelming sense of responsibility for what was a unique moment in the CIA's history: rather than supporting other agencies fighting wars, as it had done in Vietnam, or helping guerrillas fight Soviet proxy states overseas, the CIA was now fighting its own war, based on intelligence, against a terror group that was too elusive for conventional military tools. "The nation forgave us for the first round," he said, in explaining the post-9/11 choices about approving interrogation tactics. "They wouldn't forgive the second."

Long after, many former CIA officers contrast what they see as a Washington-based vilification of what they did in the Program with what they've heard personally from everyday Americans. Almost all report positive reactions from this; if anything, CIA officials who comment now—and many do not, or do rarely—are surprised at the level of support. Their audience sample is biased, but they report little or no opposition or vitriol. CIA officials feel vindicated by the response they saw among everyday Americans after the Senate report appeared. "When I speak in public," says one former Program overseer, "many [Americans] don't see it as a moral question. They see it in practical terms. Was it effective?"

They also say they have heard puzzled reactions to the Senate report after its release in 2014, and debates in Washington about the Program. One senior officer who questions some aspects of the Program nonetheless is categorical about the information the detainees provided. "I don't understand the utility debate," he says, reflecting the view of almost all officers who were there. "We were on the back foot through 2004," says a CIA executive. The detainees helped bridge the vast knowledge gap. He adds, "They [later congressional critics] could have tabled their concerns in a letter to the DCI or a letter to the president. None did. I hope nobody's ever in that position again."

The effectiveness debate hinges partly on how CIA officers judge detainee reports and how some of the American public perceives the validity of information obtained from harsh tactics. In the public debate, some critics would claim that detainees lie under duress, and that prisoners will say almost anything to assuage interrogators. Detainees, in other words, will offer up what they think their captors want.

CIA overseers of the Program have a different perspective: all detainees lie. Detainees who are not subjected to duress lie, just like al-Qa'ida prisoners at black sites. Interrogators have a few advantages in slowly weeding out lies that the public-utility debate discounts. If the interrogation team has sufficient data on a detainee—for example, the nature of the detainees' contacts with other al-Qa'ida members—the team can withhold that information over time to determine whether the detainee will offer it. If the detainee begins to provide sensitive information that the team can validate—for example, admissions about contacts with other al-Qa'ida members when the detainee is unaware that the interrogators already know of these contacts—an interrogation team might begin to assess that the detainee is at least partly compliant. Further, as the detainee pool expanded, interrogators could compare answers from multiple detainees to study which responses were consistent and which were outliers, and possibly untruthful.

Even if the Program not been revealed, or opposed, most CIA officers interviewed for this book do not believe that the Program, or any operation like it, should exist in perpetuity, or that techniques like those applied by the Agency should be a standard element in interrogations by the CIA or other agencies. These techniques, in their view, should be restricted to extreme periods in history, if used at all. Speaking a decade later, with al-Qa'ida decimated and an international coalition fighting collectively to destroy ISIS, they do not believe these techniques are appropriate, or necessary.

Under any future scenario, though, CIA officers all judge that the Agency would seek a level of clearly stated, written approval, and continued authorizations, by political leaders, including both the executive and legislative branches. They do not believe that the uproar surrounding the revelation of the techniques, including the Senate report that described these techniques as torture—the Senate study itself is known popularly as the "torture report"—would deter future Agency leaders from developing a similar program if America faced another catastrophic attack. They do, however, show an edge of bitterness in the comments by some officials, not about the CIA—as one interrogator said, "The CIA didn't throw me under the bus"—but about broader Washington, particularly the Congress. And they resent what they viewed as a too casual condemnation by President Barack Obama— "We tortured some folks"—about a Program that had received legal authorization just years before. For them, this was just another in the long line of political changes that led the new team in town to take what the former team had offered and use the Agency in a political debate between Congress and the president.

Beyond the American debates, however, senior Agency officials today lament that the US government failed to protect partners who took the risk of hosting secret facilities during those post-9/11 years. Several talk of receiving phone calls from senior foreign counterparts when revelations about locations began appearing in media around the globe. CIA officials felt a personal bond with these partners, partly because of the risk and the tight relationships they built after the attacks. "We had spent years telling them to trust us," says one operator with decades of experience managing relationships with foreign partners. Among many former Agency officials, though, the revelations were inevitable. Secrets never stay secret; there is almost nothing they remember, from the covert activities of those early years, that has not reached the public. In the eyes of many, it's the cost of doing business in a democratic society.

Those CIA officers now believe they were naïve in thinking that a national front that included the public, the Congress, and the executive branch would endure longer than it did. "If you could have captured that world support in 2002, you could have done anything," one senior operations officer recalls. "It was washed away by Iraq. Instead of the aggrieved, we became the aggressor, in the eyes of the world. We were no longer seen as universally justified." That fraying of an informal but nonethe-

less committed global coalition had begun, with striking consequences for the Program.

Today, there is universal criticism, sometimes bordering on
disgust, of congressional critiques of the Program. No officer
sees the critiques as credible; some point to the work of the 9/11
Commission, a decade earlier, as a blueprint for how to conduct a tough after-action report. That report was painful for the
Agency—bringing to light, for example, information-sharing
flaws that seemed glaring in the aftermath of the attacks—but
it is seen as a serious effort to review a turning point in the history of American intelligence. One former senior manager from
the Counterterrorism Center contrasts the two congressional
approaches—the 9/11 report and the competing Senate studies
on the Program—by highlighting three substantial differences:

- The 9/11 investigators interviewed CIA staff; the Senate
  investigators of the Program did not;
- The 9/11 investigators added recommendations for how
  the intelligence community could address some of the
  problems the report raised; the Senate investigators of the
  Program did not; and
- The 9/11 investigators published a bipartisan study; the
  Senate investigators of the Program, with two competing reports (broken down, unsurprisingly, along partisan
  lines), did not.

These Congressional briefings are now viewed by CIA officers from that era as reflecting one of the key errors of the entire
Program. The CIA prides itself on ingenuity, agility, and a general will and capability to turn on a dime to accomplish a mission.
It is not always a tightly managed organization, though, and pre-

cise policies and procedures are not Agency hallmarks. During the many congressional briefings, the CIA's Office of Congressional Affairs did not always maintain extensive notes. Further, side conversations before or after these briefings between members of the House and Senate, and their staffs, and CIA briefings often weren't well documented.

Polling about Americans' attitudes on the CIA's interrogation tactics, conducted after the release of the Senate report, play into CIA officers' views that what they did reflected the will of the American people. Pew Research Center polling from December 2014, in the wake of the Senate's release of two reports, showed 51 percent of Americans judging the CIA's tactics as justified, with 29 percent viewing the tactics as unjustified. Many CIA officers say they see this split when they speak with everyday Americans today.

Beyond the few regrets Program participants speak about from those years of detention and interrogation, almost all of them at a higher level speak of their pride in their pursuit of al-Qa'ida, and particularly in the fact that the group never succeeded in conducting another catastrophic attack in America. Eighteen years after 9/11, CIA officers from the post-attack era point to the whole range of aggressive actions—the remarkably rapid ouster of the Taliban after concerns initially about a quagmire in the Fall of 2001, the cooperation of an informal global network of intelligence services, the flood of resources into Langley, the engagement of every arm of the US government, from the president on down—as critical to gutting the al-Qa'ida threat. They not only believe they kept America safe, but also that the Program was a central piece of this puzzle. Many would say that weighing one action against the others is impossible; which was most important and which least is not clear.

Without the Program, though, most believe that another attack would have been more likely.

Overall, most Agency leaders and participants in the Program see themselves as part of a larger fight that no one—including themselves—thought they could win back in 2001. They wanted to take the remarkably broad legal and policy guidance they had and act as aggressively as they could, touching the edges of the law without crossing the line. The Program, in their eyes, was part of a broader array of US government activities, from the Afghan invasion to NSA's collection of US citizens' phone data, that prevented what seemed inevitable during the early 2000s: the Second Wave. They all believe the Program contributed to that success, though they differ on the extent of the Program's contribution. And they are all proud to have participated in a fight that they believe succeeded because they pushed the limits. Later critiques never diminished that sense among them. In the words of one high-ranking official from that era, summing up what seemed after 9/11 like a fight against al-Qa'ida against long odds, "We won."